WESLEY: APOSTOLIC MAN

WESLEY: APOSTOLIC MAN

*Some Reflections on Wesley's
Consecration of Dr Thomas Coke*

by
EDGAR W. THOMPSON

WIPF & STOCK · Eugene, Oregon

Wipf and Stock Publishers
199 W 8th Ave, Suite 3
Eugene, OR 97401

Wesley: Apostolic Man
Some Reflections on Wesley's Consecration
of Dr. Thomas Coke
By Thompson, Edgar W.
Copyright©1957 Methodist Publishing - Epworth Press
ISBN 13: 978-1-4982-0713-3
Publication date 10/15/2014
Previously published by Epworth Press, 1957

CONTENTS

CHAPTER I

THE CONSECRATION

OF all the 'irregularities' of John Wesley, from an Anglican point of view, his setting apart of Dr Thomas Coke as a Superintendent was outstanding and most to be deplored: it was nothing other than the consecration of Coke for a bishopric in America. There are two reasons why a fresh consideration of this act is timely.

First, under the Scheme of Union for North India for the first time in history a large section of the Methodist Episcopal Church of America may assent to unite organically with Churches of another denomination, episcopal and non-episcopal; and it has been necessary to determine and to agree how to deal with the American bishops, whose succession is from Dr Coke. The North Indian Scheme, unlike the South Indian, proposes that there shall be from the beginning a unification of the several Ministries, including the Episcopate.

For all the bishops of North India, whether Anglican or Methodist Episcopal, union will mean entrance into a wider jurisdiction and a more varied fellowship. At least three bishops of the Historic Episcopate, that is, 'the Episcopate which is in historic continuity with that of the early Church', will lay their hands upon the American bishops and commission them for their new and greater office with the words:

'Forasmuch as thou wast called and duly appointed within the Methodist Episcopal Church to the office of a Bishop in the Church of God, and art now called to the office of a Bishop in the Church of God within the united Church, mayest thou receive from God the grace of the Holy Spirit for the further exercise of God's ministry in the office of a Bishop—in the name of the Father, and of the Son, and of the Holy Ghost.

And, in their turn the American bishops will take part in laying their hands upon the Anglican bishops, offering the same prayer, with the necessary alteration of words, over them and giving to them the same extended authority.

There is here no pronouncement upon the nature of the

American Episcopate—no indication of any limitation or imperfection in it; but the purpose is that by this common service of consecration, the American bishops shall be supplied with 'that special link with the Episcopate of the Primitive Church which the Anglican Communion claims to have preserved', and shall secure a Ministry fully accredited in the eyes of all the members of the united Church.[1]

Secondly, the Conference of the Methodist Church last year was informed that the Synods of the two Anglican Convocations had requested the Archbishops to open conversations with the Methodist Church on the basis of the Report on *Church Relations*. The Methodist Conference responded gladly to this overture and empowered the President to appoint delegates, if and when an invitation to such conversations was received. It is common knowledge that the Episcopate will be the principal matter to be discussed in any conversation between the two Churches. It will be of benefit for Methodists to consider afresh all the issues which are involved in Wesley's consecration of Coke, seeing clearly where they stand; and also that Anglicans should know what are the principles of Church Order to which the Methodist Church has committed itself.

On 1st September 1784, John Wesley was staying as a guest in the house of Mr Castleman, 6 Dighton Street, King's Square, Bristol. There in one of the rooms, being assisted by James Creighton and Thomas Coke, like himself presbyters of the Church of England, he ordained at the early hour of 4 a.m. Richard Whatcoat and Thomas Vasey for service as deacons among the Methodists of the United States of America. On the following morning, with the same assistance and at the same hour, he ordained them as elders. Afterwards with the assistance of James Creighton and the two newly ordained elders, Whatcoat and Vasey, he set apart Dr Coke as Superintendent among the American Methodists, to supply them with ministers and the sacraments—or, in other words, Wesley consecrated Coke to the office of bishop.

We must suppose, I think, that Whatcoat and Vasey took part in this consecration, because there were only three

[1] *Plan of Church Union in North India and Pakistan.*

presbyters of the Church of England present in these acts of ordination, Wesley, Coke, and Creighton, and when Coke was being consecrated, there would be left only one presbyter of the Church of England, James Creighton, to assist Wesley. He speaks, however, in his certificate of ordination, of 'being assisted by other ordained ministers'. Perhaps it is significant that he does not call them presbyters of the Church of England, but simply 'ordained ministers'. If Whatcoat and Vasey were now 'Elders' or presbyters of the American Church, it was fitting that they should unite with Creighton in laying hands on Coke.

Doubtless in all these Services of Ordination, Wesley used the forms which he had already drawn up. They were in substance taken from that Liturgy of the Church of England which he so greatly loved—from the 'Form and Manner of Making of Deacons, the Ordering of Priests, and the Ordaining or Consecration of Bishops'. These forms Coke took with him to America, and they were immediately published in America in *The Sunday Service of the Methodists in the United States of America.*

A few days later Coke, Whatcoat and Vasey sailed from Bristol for the United States.

Wesley, as Coke desired, gave to him a certificate of his consecration, and in explanation of his plan Wesley addressed a general letter to 'Our Brethren in America'. These are foundation documents and constitute the Charter of the American Methodist Episcopal Church.

The first, as is fitting, is preserved in the archives of the Methodist Missionary Society at Marylebone Road, London, for Coke was not only a bishop of the American Episcopal Church, he was also for nearly thirty years—until his death at sea on the way to India—the General Superintendent of the Foreign Missions begun and supported by the British Conference. The certificate ran as below. In the standard works of Tyerman, Smith, and Simon, it is printed with some slight inaccuracies. It is here quoted with Wesley's spelling and use of capitals as in the original document (a professed facsimile appears in Curnock's Standard Edition of the *Journal*, Vol. VII, p. 16: even this contains one error).

THE ORDINATION CERTIFICATE

To all to whom these Presents shall come, John Wesley, late Fellow of Lincoln College in Oxford, Presbyter of the Church of England, sendeth greeting.

Whereas many of the People in the Southern Provinces of North America who desire to continue under my care, and still adhere to the Doctrines and Discipline of the Church of England are greatly distrest for want of Ministers to administer the Sacraments of Baptism and the Lord's Supper according to the usage of the said Church: And whereas there does not appear to be any other way of Supplying them with Ministers:

Know all men, that I John Wesley think myself to be providentially called at this time to set apart some persons for the work of the ministry in America. And therefore under the Protection of Almighty God, and with a single eye to his Glory, I have this day set apart as a Superintendent, by the imposition of my hands and prayer, (being assisted by other ordained Ministers) Thomas Coke, Doctor of Civil Law, a Presbyter of the Church of England, and a man whom I judge to be well qualified for that great work. And I do hereby recommend him to all whom it may concern as a fit person to preside over the Flock of Christ. In testimony whereof I have hereunto set my hand and seal this second day of September in the year of our Lord one thousand seven hundred and eighty four

JOHN WESLEY

The letter to America is dated 10th September 1784 from Bristol, and reads as follows:

THE LETTER TO THE AMERICAN BRETHREN
To Dr Coke, Mr Asbury and our Brethren in North America

1. By a very uncommon train of providences many of the Provinces of North America are totally disjoined from their Mother Country and created into independent States. The English Government has no authority over them, either civil or ecclesiastical, any more than over the States of Holland. A civil authority is exercised over them, partly by the Congress, partly by the Provincial Assemblies. But no one either exercises or claims any ecclesiastical authority at all. In this particular situation some thousands of the inhabitants of these States desire my advice; and in compliance with their desire I have drawn up a little sketch.

2. Lord King's *Account of the Primitive Church* convinced me many years ago that bishops and presbyters are the same order, and consequently have the same right to ordain. For many years I have been importuned from time to time to exercise this right by ordaining part of our travelling preachers. But I have still refused, not only for peace' sake, but because I was determined as little as possible to violate the established order of the National Church to which I belonged.

3. But the case is widely different between England and North America. Here there are bishops who have a legal jurisdiction: in America there are none, neither any parish ministers. So that for some hundred miles together there is none either to baptize or to administer the Lord's Supper. Here, therefore, my scruples are at an end; and I conceive myself at full liberty, as I violate no order and invade no man's right by appointing and sending labourers into the harvest.

4. I have accordingly appointed Dr Coke and Mr Francis Asbury to be Joint Superintendents over our brethren in North America; as also Richard Whatcoat and Thomas Vasey to act as elders among them, by baptizing and administering the Lord's Supper. And I have prepared a Liturgy little differing from that of the Church of England (I think the best constituted National Church in the world) which I advise all the travelling preachers to use on the Lord's Day in all the congregations, reading the Litany only on Wednesdays and Fridays and praying extempore on all other days. I also advise the elders to administer the Supper of the Lord on every Lord's Day.

5. If any one will point out to me a more rational and scriptural way of feeding and guiding those poor sheep in the wilderness, I will gladly embrace it. At present I cannot see any better method than that I have taken.

6. It has, indeed, been proposed to desire the English bishops to ordain part of our preachers for America. But to this I object;

(1) I desired the Bishop of London to ordain only one, but could not prevail. (2) If they consented, we know the slowness of their proceedings; but the matter admits of no delay. (3) If they would ordain them now, they would likewise expect to govern them. And how grievously would this entangle us! (4) As our American brethren are now totally disentangled both from the State and from the English hierarchy, we dare not entangle them again either with the one or the other. They are now at full liberty simply to follow the Scriptures and the Primitive Church. And we judge it best that they should stand fast in that liberty wherewith God has so strangely made them free.[2]

We will deal here with only one point—whose was the responsibility for this plan? On Wesley's death seven years later, the first biography of him, after some controversy about the issue of it, was published by Dr Whitehead. He had been Wesley's physician, and, in Marshall Cluxton's Academy picture of 'The Death Bed of John Wesley', he is the tall cloaked figure in the extreme right foreground, looking down upon the scene. Whitehead denounced the whole transaction of

[2] *Letters of John Wesley* (Standard Edn), VII.238-9.

Coke's ordination as a mere hotch-potch of inconsistencies, and declared his belief that Wesley would never have adopted so mis-shapen a plan, had not his clear perception of things been rendered feeble and dim by 'flattery, persuasion, and age'.

But Wesley in 1784 was feeling particularly well. At the beginning of the year he refers to some of the weaknesses of his youth, and recounts: 'By the blessing of God, I have outlived them all. I have no infirmities now.' He undertook the most extensive travels in England and Scotland, and a man who could trudge twelve and a half miles on foot through heavy Scottish rain, and be 'no more tired at the end than when he set out' can hardly be written off as senile. And there is no sign of the decay of his mental powers in the correspondence of the period. Whether or not we can accept Wesley's letter to America as a sufficient *Apologia* for his action, we cannot fail to admire the lucidity, cogency, and compactness of its thought and expression. The truth is that Wesley in his eighty-second year still was an extraordinarily fit and able man.

And as for being persuaded or overborne by others—Coke and the Methodist preachers—the facts are altogether against the supposition. When Wesley first broached this matter to Coke in February 1784, Coke's mind was set upon leading a mission to India, and it was necessary for Wesley to dissuade him from that project and to convince him that the need and opportunity of the Far West were greater, at that time, than those of the Far East. It is true that Coke in a letter of 9th August 1784, when Wesley had resolved upon his plan, wrote to him suggesting that, inasmuch as he was to be sent out to America 'with the power of ordaining others', or 'to exercise the office of ordination', it would be well for him to receive this power by the imposition of Wesley's hands, that there might be no question about his position and authority in America.

Coke, I fear, cannot always be acquitted of personal ambition, but in view of Wesley's proposal for himself, this was a just and reasonable request.

The other Methodist preachers whom Wesley consulted about his plan for America were astonished and disapproved when they heard of it. One of them, Pawson, wrote: 'I plainly saw it would be done, as Mr Wesley's mind appeared to be quite made up.'[3]

No, we cannot lay the responsibility for this act on any other person than John Wesley himself. He would not have sought to put the burden upon another, but would have taken it readily and with a good conscience upon his own shoulders. John Wesley did not consult or even inform his brother Charles of what he intended to do; for he knew well that his brother would be inflexibly opposed to his way of providing for the spiritual needs of American Methodists. The entry in his *Journal* for 1st September 1784, is 'Being now clear in my own mind, I took a step which I had long weighed in my mind'.

In the following March, when the results of his action were beginning to appear, he wrote to one of his preachers, Barnabas Thomas

DEAR BARNABAS,

I have neither inclination nor leisure to draw the saw of controversy; but I will tell you my mind in a few words.

I am now as firmly attached to the Church of England as I ever was since you knew me. But meantime I know myself to be as real a Christian bishop as the Archbishop of Canterbury. Yet I was always resolved, and am so still, never to act as such except in case of necessity. Such a case does not (perhaps never will) exist in England. In America it did exist. This I made known to the Bishop of London and desired his help. But he peremptorily refused it. All the other bishops were of the same mind; the rather because (they said) they had nothing to do with America. Then I saw my way clear, and was fully convinced what it was my duty to do. As to the persons amongst those who offered themselves I chose those whom I judged most worthy, and I positively refuse to be judged herein by any man's conscience but my own.[4]

Right or wrong, these are not the words of an old man in senile decay, incapable of making up his own mind, and lamenting that others had made it up for him. One cannot help remarking, however, that the time soon came when Wesley ordained for Scotland, and then for England. The ordinations of Whatcoat, Vasey, and Coke in 1784 were the first in a series of ordinations by Wesley of which the last recorded were in 1789.

[3] Tyerman, III.428.   [4] *Letters*, VII.262.

CHAPTER II

THE RULE OF SCRIPTURE

FOUR elements or principles can be distinguished in the spiritual composition and churchmanship of John Wesley:

(1) Acceptance of the Holy Scriptures as the Rule of Faith and Practice;
(2) Reverence for the usages of the Primitive Church;
(3) A warm and unquenchable love for the Church of England, and especially for her Doctrines and Liturgy, as these are to be found in the *Book of Common Prayer* and the *Homilies*;
(4) A constant and unshakable conviction that God had commanded him to proclaim the Good News of Salvation to all whom he could reach, and had appointed him to care for the souls of those who were converted under the preaching of himself and his 'Helpers'.

It is impossible to read the *Letters* and *Journals* of Wesley, his *Sermons* and apologetic writings, without finding again and again these principles operative in his mind. The first and the last he regards as immutable, always to be obeyed: about the second and the third he is sometimes in doubt and hesitant. There may be an inner conflict, a period of strain and stress, until he has decided which principle he must set aside and which follow. He was, as we shall see, often at his wits' end to say what was the Church of England, and what should be contained in his allegiance to her.

'Child', said my father to me when I was young, 'you think to carry everything by dint of argument. But you will find by-and-by how very little is ever done in the world by clear reason.' Very little indeed![1]

Wesley imagined that he had grown out of his boyish illusion: he never did. The child was the father of the man: hence *His Appeals to Men of Reason*. To the very end he trusted that there was in all other men an active principle of reasonableness,

[1] *Letters*, V.203; to Joseph Benson.

ready to be convinced by valid argument. And so also he sought to preserve in himself an intellectual conscience to which no truth could appeal in vain. After he has declared in the strongest terms his own opinions, he often asks his reader to correct him, if in anything he has erred. This is not a pose; it is the attitude of one who was sincere and open-minded, and always anxious to be brought nearer to truth. Because Wesley was such a man, his beliefs and words are not always consistent. The reasonable man does not remain for ever in one stance; he moves on. That is why it is so important in quoting John Wesley to show when and where he said anything, and why he said it. But after all Wesley was human and suffered from our common infirmities. It may seem to us that there were occasions when he adhered obstinately to his own opinion against the better reason; and that one such occasion was when he failed to face the searching questions of his brother Charles about the consecration of Coke.

Let us turn first to the Scriptures. Wesley believed that they contained the Rule of Faith. Nothing was to be taught or required of any man as necessary to salvation but what can be proved by Scripture. He found in Holy Writ—through Jesus Christ, the Word of God—the passage from death unto life, the way of repentance and faith, pardon and sanctification; but he did not find there a pattern of Church government to be preserved and reproduced always and everywhere. He did not define the Church by its mode of organization or its constitution as a society. Taking as his text Ephesians 4$^{1-6}$ he said from the pulpit:

The Catholic or Universal Church is all the persons in the Universe whom God hath so called out of the world as to entitle them to the preceding character—as to be 'one Body', united by 'one Spirit', having 'one faith, one hope, one baptism, one God and Father of all, who is above and through all and in them all'.

This account is exactly agreeable to the Nineteenth Article of our Church, the Church of England; 'The visible Church of Christ is a congregation of faithful men in which the pure word of God is preached, and the sacraments be duly administered.' It may be observed that, at the same time our Thirty-Nine Articles were compiled and published, a Latin translation of them was published by the same. In this the words were *'coetus credentium'*,[2] 'a congregation of believers', plainly showing that by *faithful men* the compilers meant men endued with living faith.

Wesley might have quoted as a shorter definition of the Church, coming nearer in agreement to the account given by the Apostle, the beautiful phrase in the alternative prayer of the Communion Service: *'the mystical Body of Thy Son, which is the blessed company of all faithful people'*. What is important for us to observe is that Wesley defines the Church not by the form of its government, but by the faith and life of its members. Here the content of the definition is positive, but elsewhere he has put forward clearly the negative aspect. He did not equate Faith with Order.

We shall see later that John Wesley had not always held this view of Church government, though it came to him very early in the Methodist movement. At the Annual Conference, held in London in 1747, which was only the fourth in the series, we find the following entries in the *Minutes*:

Q. Are the three Orders of Bishops, Priests, and Deacons plainly described in the New Testament?

A. We think they are, and believe they generally obtained in the churches of the Apostolic Age.

Q. But are you assured God designs the same plan should obtain in all Churches throughout all ages?

A. We are not assured of this, because we do not know that it is asserted in Holy Writ.

Q. If this plan were essential to a Christian Church, what must become of all the foreign Reformed Churches?

A. It would follow, they are no parts of the Church of Christ—a consequence full of shocking absurdity.

Q. In what age was the divine right of Episcopacy first asserted in England?

A. About the middle of Queen Elizabeth's reign. Till then all the bishops and clergy in England continually allowed and joined in the ministrations of those who were not episcopally ordained.

Q. Must there not be numberless accidental variations in the government of various Churches?

A. There must be, in the nature of things. As God variously dispenses His gifts of nature, providence, and grace, both the

---

[2] Wesley's memory seems to have been at fault. The Latin is *coetus fidelium*—'the company of the faithful,' of those who are true to the Faith. The 'faithful' (*fideles*) are much more than 'the believers' (*credentes*). They are those who have kept the Faith, and added conduct to creed.

offices themselves and the officers in each ought to be varied from time to time.

Q. *Why is it that there is no determinate plan of Church government appointed in Scripture?*

A. Without doubt, because the wisdom of God had a regard to the necessary variety.

Q. *Was there any thought of uniformity in the government of all Churches until the time of Constantine?*

A. It is certain there was not; and would not have been, had men consulted the Word of God only.

We are not concerned with the correctness of the views of ecclesiastical history exhibited here. Our purpose is to show how clearly and strongly Wesley held that no particular form of Church government is enjoined by Scripture and none can claim to be of sole Divine Right. The Church cannot be defined by its form of government.

There are two writers on Church government who are principally quoted by Wesley in connexion with his ordination of Coke. They are Bishop Stillingfleet and Lord King. It will be necessary to refer to both in more detail later on; but, at this point, it is worth noting that both of them were very young men when they wrote their books, and they had all the ardour and generous feelings of youth. They were shocked at the disunity of Christians in the England of their time, and at the bitterness of denominational strife. Both of them put forward a plea for unity and intended their books to be a healing of division.

Stillingfleet was twenty-four years of age when his *Irenicum* was published in 1656. The controversies among Presbyterians, Independents, and Episcopalians were then drawing to a climax. He was at that time Rector of Sutton, and after the Restoration rose to great dignities in the Church of England, becoming Dean of St Paul's and Bishop of Worcester. It is said that he repented some injudicious expressions in his *Irenicum*, but he never recanted its main theme. Indeed, he could not, without withdrawing and repudiating the entire book.

There is a sort of opulence and splendour in Stillingfleet's prose—a rich after-glow of Elizabethan literature. He begins his Preface to the Reader with these words:

B

I write not to increase the controversies of the times, nor to foment the differences that are among us, the one are by far too many, the other too great already. My only design is to allay the heat, and abate the fury of that *Ignis sacer*, or Erysipelas of contention, which hath risen in the face of our Church . . . and although with the poor Persian I can only bring a hand-full of water, yet that may be my just Apology, that it is for the quenching these flames in the Church which have caused the bells of Aaron to jangle so much, that it seems to be a work of the greatest difficulty to make them tunable.

Stillingfleet sought to prove that no form of Church government—Independent, Presbyterian, or Episcopal, could claim to possess a *Jus Divinum*. Our Lord had not instituted a particular Church Order, and left His commandment about it. The notices in the New Testament about the government set up by the Apostles in various churches were so scanty that we cannot be sure what precisely it was: and in any case, Scripture does not make it obligatory for all time. He sums up his purpose in the writing of his great book in the sentence:

This hath been the whole design of this Treatise to prove that the Form of Church Government is a mere matter of Prudence, regulated by the Word of God.

He sought to show that in the early Church there were progressive changes in the form of government, and that the object of these was always to promote Christian living, and to advance the peace and unity of the Church of God. He thought that, by the corruption of the Church in his own time, some excellencies of primitive government had been mutilated or lost, and he desired that they should be restored by a plan of comprehension. He wrote, in words that might have been adopted as a motto by the framers of the Constitution of the Church of South India:

All parties may retain their opinions concerning the Primitive form, and yet agree and pitch upon a form compounded of all together as the most suitable to the state and condition of the Church of God among us: That so the peoples interest be secured by consent and suffrage, which is the pretence of the Congregational way; the due power of Presbyteries asserted by their joint concurrence with the Bishop; and the just honour and dignity of the Bishop asserted, as a very laudable and ancient constitution for preserving the peace and unity of the Church of God.

To which we may add, as a reform desired by Stillingfleet:

The contracting of Dioceses into such a compass as may be fitted for the personal inspection of the Bishop, the constant preaching of the Bishop and residence in his Diocese.

I have quoted Stillingfleet at some length, because he seems to me to have had a much wider and more enduring influence on Wesley than Peter King. He laid down a principle of far-reaching consequence—that the form of Church government has not been determined by specific injunctions of Holy Writ, but may be found in the succeeding ages in what has made for the spiritual welfare of the Church and has created and preserved its unity and peace. This was the foundation of the pragmatism in Wesley's churchmanship. The *Irenicum*, like some other works of Stillingfleet, is a big book of immense erudition, amazing in one so young. In the atmosphere created by this great-hearted and learned man, Wesley's thought breathed and took shape.

The form of Church government, he—like Stillingfleet—believed, must be such as to serve the purposes of the Church; it must be the instrument of faith and life alike for the Christian individual and for the Christian community. To this end it was necessary that it should be 'agreeable to Scripture and the Apostles' teaching'. How completely in the spirit of Stillingfleet are the words in Wesley's letter to America:

If any one will point out a more *rational and scriptural* way of feeding and guiding those poor sheep in the wilderness, I will gladly embrace it. At present I cannot see a better method than that I have taken.

Wesley, therefore, thought that we look in vain in Scripture for an inflexible and universal rule of Church government. Christ gave no commandments about it, and the New Testament does not exhibit a clearly defined and invariable pattern of the organization of the Church. That is a matter which the Lord of the Church has remitted to the care and judgement of His faithful people; and, in so far as they are faithful, they will not lack His guidance and approval. Church Order thus will accord both with the Divine will and with human reason. In Wesley's view the sole divine right of Episcopacy, or of any other form of Church government, is not among the things that may be read in Scripture or may be proved thereby, and therefore it is not to be required of any man that it should be believed as an Article of the Faith, or be thought necessary to salvation.

This is a view which has been held by many members of the Church of England—its bishops, clergy and laity, from the Reformation down to the present day; and Wesley, as a priest of the English Church, was perfectly entitled to profess it. He found support for it directly in the works of an eminent Anglican bishop and divine.

CHAPTER III

THE USAGES OF THE PRIMITIVE CHURCH

WE come now to the second element in Wesley's church-manship—his reverence for the usages of the Primitive Church. What is the instinct within us producing a special regard for that which is early in the institutions and the practice of the Church? Whatever it be, Wesley shared it to the full. He felt, with us, that the nearer the water is to its source, the purer is it likely to be. In the perplexity into which he was thrown by the American situation, he looked into the past for precedents to guide him. It is a habit which should encourage innovation as well as conservation—the striking out of a new path as well as the following of an old one; for the most ancient precedent was once an innovation. The minds of religious teachers may become so cluttered up with precedents that they lose the power of decision and action, fail to see a situation in its urgency and are powerless to deal with it. It was so among the Scribes in Jewry, and it has been so among ecclesiastics in Christendom.

Wesley was no mean Patristic scholar. He was well read in the Apostolic Fathers and the greatest Fathers of the later age. In his address to the English clergy, he proposed that they should examine themselves, and among other questions ask:

Am I acquainted with the Fathers; at least with those venerable men in the earliest ages of the Church? Have I read over and over again the golden remains of Clemens Romanus, of Ignatius and Polycarp; and have I given one reading at least, to the works of Justin Martyr, Tertullian, Origen, Clemens Alexandrinus, and Cyprian?

Wesley would not propose any test to his fellow clergy to which he had not first submitted himself. We can be sure that, if he regarded the reading of the Fathers as the duty of a clergyman, it was a study in which he himself had been diligent. Elsewhere he adds to this list the great Post-Nicene Fathers—Basil, Chrysostom, Ephraim Syrus (the man of 'the broken heart'), and Augustine.

Yet Wesley did not resort to the Fathers primarily to settle questions of ecclesiastical order. He sought in them the evidences of genuine Christianity. He says that when he was on his way to Rotterdam he was much pressed to take notice of a book published in 1748 by Dr Middleton, Fellow of Trinity College, Cambridge, in which the credulity of the Fathers of the primitive Church in believing and promulgating idle stories of spurious miracles, was severely castigated. Wesley postponed his voyage, sat down in London, and within twenty days wrote a Reply to Middleton, which occupies more than 70 pages in the Standard Edition of the *Letters*.[1] Wesley thought that some of the Apostolic Fathers were men of little learning and weak understanding, and that they held opinions which could not now be defended—

And yet I exceedingly reverence them as well as their writings, and esteem them very highly in love. I reverence them because they were Christians. . . . And I reverence their writings, because they describe true, genuine Christianity, and direct us to the strongest evidence of the Christian doctrine. Indeed, in addressing the heathens of those times, they intermix other arguments [drawn from miracles] . . . . But still they never relinquish this: 'What the Scripture promises, I enjoy. Come and see what Christianity has done here, and acknowledge it is of God.' I reverence these ancient Christians (with all their failings) the more, because I see so few Christians now.

But when Wesley was confronted with the situation in the United States of America, he did turn to the Primitive Church and the Apostolic Fathers for guidance in Church government. What was he to do? What would they have done, had they been in like case? In North America the Methodists, under Wesley's direction, had followed the same plan as in the British Isles. They heard the Word of God from their travelling preachers and found fellowship in the meetings of their Societies, but for worship and the sacraments they were to go to the parish churches. As a consequence of the War of Independence, most of the Anglican clergy, with their English sympathies and loyalty, had fled; and the churches were left deserted, so that 'for some hundred miles together, there is none either to baptize or to administer the Lord's Supper'. How was this lack of a Christian ministry to be supplied?

[1] II.312-88.

In his anxious and prolonged deliberations Wesley recalled a book which had effected, nearly forty years before, a revolution in his views about the Ministry in the Church. He and his brother Charles had received a letter from their profligate brother-in-law, Westley Hall, denouncing them for their ecclesiastical beliefs and requiring them to leave the Church of England. John says that he wrote a reply, dated 30th December 1745, on behalf of Charles and himself. It expresses High Church views in their most rigid and extreme form, and one cannot help wondering whether, though the signature is John's, Charles had not more to do with the wording of the letter. However that may be, this confession of dogmatic faith contains the following clauses:

We believe it would not be right for us to administer either Baptism or the Lord's Supper unless we had a commission so to do from those bishops whom we apprehend to be in a succession from the Apostles. And yet we allow these bishops are the successors of those who were dependent on the Bishop of Rome.

We believe there is, and always was, in every Christian Church (whether dependent on the Bishop of Rome or not) an outward priesthood, ordained by Jesus Christ, and an outward sacrifice offered therein, by men authorized to act as ambassadors of Christ and stewards of the mysteries of God.

We believe that the threefold order of ministers is not only authorized by its apostolical institution, but also by the Written Word.[2]

Three weeks later, he is on the road for Bristol, and he carries in his saddle-bags a little book by Peter King entitled *An Enquiry into the Constitution, Discipline, Unity and Worship of the Primitive Church, That Flourished within the first Three Hundred Years after Christ, Faithfully Collected out of the Extant Writings of those Ages—By an Impartial Hand.*

It was published in 1691, when its author was only twenty-two years of age. Stillingfleet's book was issued to make peace when the controversy was raging among Independents, Presbyterians and Episcopalians in the time of the Commonwealth before the Restoration. King's book was also issued with peaceful intent, this time, after the Restoration when the harsh settlement of the Act of Uniformity had been made in 1662, and the Five Mile and Conventicle Acts had cut short the liberties of Dissenters. After the Revolution under William and Mary the Toleration Act of 1689 made a partial restoration of the liberty to worship God according to conscience. Our school histories mention these facts, and most of us have some acquaintance with them: but they do not show that, immediately after the passing of the Act of Toleration, the king appointed a Commission of Bishops and Clergy to revise the *Book of Common Prayer* and the *Canons*, making such changes as the exigencies of the time required. It seemed as though the opportunity for recovering unity in English Christianity, lost in 1662, had recurred. Men like Bishop Tillotson were eager to advance to a comprehension of Dissenters, and alterations were drafted which probably would have satisfied and would have been accepted by them. But the Convocations declined even to consider these proposals, and another opportunity for reunion passed away unused and fruitless. All this was fresh in the mind of the young Peter King when he took up his pen; the turmoil and controversies had not yet died down. He himself was of Nonconformist antecedents and was educated in a Dissenting academy, but he afterwards joined the Church of England and rose to great eminence in civil life, being made Lord Chancellor and Baron of Ockham in Surrey. His book was published anonymously, but later both it and the author's name became well known. The writer of the notice of Lord King in the *Dictionary of National Biography* says that his work was recognized as the authoritative text-book for the period until the publication of Hatch's Bampton lectures.

There is a very pleasing candour and modesty in his approach to his subject: He writes in his preface:

The design of the following Treatise is in general to represent the Constitution, Discipline, Unity and Worship of the Primitive Church, that flourished within the first Three Hundred Years after Christ; but more particularly and especially to describe their Opinions and Practices with respect to those Things that are now unhappily controverted between those of these Kingdoms, who are commonly known as Church of England-men, Presbyterians, Independents, and Anabaptists. . . .

What I have written as to this subject I have wholly collected out of the Genuine and unquestionably Authentick Writings of those

Ages, making use of no other Writings whatsoever, except the Ecclesiastical History of Eusebius. . . .

I assure the whole world our unnatural Quarrels do so much afflict and trouble me, as that I would sacrifice not only this Book, but all that I either am or have, if thereby I might be an happy Instrument to compose and heal them. But amongst other Reasons, these two were the chiefest that swayed me hereunto, To inform others what the Practices of the Primitive Apostolick Churches were; or, if I am mistaken (as who is without his Errors?) to be better informed myself; wherefore without any Ostentation or Challenging, but unfeignedly and sincerely to prevent Mistakes in my younger years I humbly desire and shall heartily thank any Learned Person, that will be so kind as to inform me, if he knows me to have erred in any one or more Particulars . . . and then I promise, if my Mistakes are fairly shewn, I will not pertinaciously and obstinately defend them, but most willingly and thankfully renounce them, since my design is not to defend a Party, but to search out the Truth.

This was the very mood to capture and subdue Wesley's judgement; and the record of that ride to Bristol reads:

On the road I read over Lord King's *Account of the Primitive Church*. In spite of the vehement prejudice of my education, I was ready to believe that this was a fair and impartial draught; but, if so, it would follow that bishops and presbyters are (essentially) of one order, and that originally every Christian congregation was a church independent on all others.

Why did Wesley publish in his *Journal* that extraordinary letter of 30th December 1745, and follow it up three weeks later with this entry of 20th January 1746? Was it that he wished to make plain to all who had an interest in him that his ecclesiastical opinions had undergone a radical change? In any case, this is not an example of Wesley's inconsistency, but of his reasonableness. This must be one of the rare cases in which an argument has converted an Anglo-Catholic. At the same time let us remember that the belief about the constitution of the Church which Wesley now renounced as erroneous had not prevented him from being for several years the most heroic and successful evangelist in our English history.

But let us come to King's book. Wesley brings it forward again in his *Apologia*, addressed to 'Our Brethren in America':

Lord King's *Account of the Primitive Church* convinced me many years ago that bishops and presbyters are the same order, and consequently have the same right to ordain.

King's book is not a large one, and it is written with such lucidity that it is easy to read. It is to me rather astonishing that among the many writers, Anglican and Methodist, who have discussed the consecration of Coke, no one ever seems to have taken the trouble to examine this work of King and determine whether it does really support the claim of Wesley. Modern scholarship assuredly will not accept King's description of the Church of the first three centuries as complete or adequate in all respects. It would say that King's account is altogether too simplified. It does barely recognize that the materials for a constitutional history of the Church in the New Testament are very scanty, and that in the apostolic and subapostolic periods there may have been varieties of organization, but the picture of the Church which King paints and leaves in the mind is of the Church as by the end of the second century, it had settled down generally into Monepiscopacy.

It is interesting to compare King's *Account of the Primitive Church* with that which has been given by a modern scholar. The late Canon Streeter's book, *The Primitive Church*, bears a similar title; but his treatment of the subject is very different. His statement is:

It is not disputed that by A.D. 200 a system of Church organization in its main structure uniform had come into existence throughout the Christian World. But the hypothesis that this uniformity of system displaced an earlier diversity, is, I submit, one that has a valid claim to serious consideration.

And again:

There follows the principle I have had occasion to emphasize—the history of Catholic Christianity during the first five centuries is the history of a progressive standardization of a diversity which had its origin in the Apostolic age.

King describes a standardized and uniform system of government in the early Church without any indication of the manner in which or the stages by which it was shaped and arrived at out of the pre-existing varieties and diversities of government.

The first point, according to King, was that the typical diocese in that early age was not a district or a provincial area, but a city parish as in the churches of Antioch or Alexandria, Rome or Carthage. The area of the bishop's diocese and the number of Christians in it were not so large but that all the members of the church could assemble as one congregation. In this parish the bishop was the chief minister with the pastoral care of the whole flock, and the presbyters were his assistants. The presbyters and bishop formed a court of the church or consistory with the bishop as president. The presbyters were ordained by the bishop, assisted by presbyters, after they had been subjected to trial and examination, and with the consent and approval of the whole congregation and presbytery. The bishop himself was appointed after election by and with the consent of the congregation, his ordination being by the hands of neighbouring bishops. King cannot discover that any number of these was fixed (remember that his period closes before the Council of Nicæa), but he thinks it probable that the number would be not less than three. He sums up the position in the words:

But, whether the Election of a Bishop be ascribed to the adjoining Ministers or to the People of the Parish, it comes all to one and the same thing: neither the Choice of the Bishops of the Voisinage, without the Consent of the People, nor the Election of the People, without the Approbation of those Bishops, was sufficient and valid of itself; but both concurred to a legal and orderly Promotion, which was according to the Example of the Apostles and Apostolick Preachers, who in the first Plantation of Churches, Ordained Bishops and Deacons with the consent of the whole Church.

When we contrast this primitive order with the existing conditions in the Church of England, the eirenic and reforming tendency of this young man's observations becomes obvious.

I have given this account of the office of the bishop in the Primitive Church according to King, in order that we may see more clearly what is the position which he assigns to the presbyters, and as soon as we come to this, we begin to tremble for John Wesley. King's definition of a presbyter runs as follows:

A Person in Holy Orders, having thereby an inherent Right to perform the whole Office of a Bishop; but being possessed of no Place or Parish, not actually discharging it, without the Permission or consent of the Bishop of a Place or Parish.

Thus King held that the presbyter had the same inherent rights with the bishop to perform all the offices of the Ministry —he could preach, baptize, administer the Lord's Supper, discipline, and ordain—but all these things he could do only with the permission of the bishop, and without his permission not one of them. So that

Presbyters were different from the Bishops *in gradu* or in Degree; but yet they were equal *in ordine* or in Order.

If, therefore, King taught that in the primitive Church there were only two orders (presbyters and deacons), he also taught that among presbyters, there were two degrees (an inferior, the ordinary presbyters, and a superior, the bishop). If presbyters were the same in order, they were not the same in degree. What was this distinction of *gradus* or degree? It was not negligible, but of great potency. The bishop possessed an authority and power which the presbyter did not. If, at his ordination, the presbyter received the right to preach and to administer the sacraments, he could only exercise these rights, as and when he was authorized so to do by the bishop. If there was such difference in *degrees*, was it not better to say with the Church of England that there were three orders in the Ministry, instead of saying with King, that there were two *orders*, with two degrees in one of them? We have to remember that King was eager to mollify and reconcile Episcopalians and Presbyterians, and this was his way of doing it.

However, we are concerned with John Wesley. It was not a sufficient and complete summary of King for him to write in 1747: 'Bishops and presbyters are (essentially) of one order.' He left out 'but of two *grades*'. He does imply by the word he put in brackets—'*essentially*', that there is some sort of difference between bishops and presbyters, but he does not indicate that the difference is as great as between *esse* and *posse*, between rights that are inherent and can be freely exercised and rights that can only be exercised with the consent of another.

It is significant that thirty-eight years later the qualifying '*essentially*' has been dropped, and Wesley wrote to America simply—'Bishops and presbyters are the same order, and consequently have the same right to ordain'; upon which King would remark: 'Presbyters have no right to ordain, except by the bishop's permission.'

With regard to the presbyter's power and practice of ordaining King writes:

As for Ordination, I find but little said of this in Antiquity; yet, as little as there is, there are clearer proofs of the Presbyters ordaining than there are of their administering the Lords' Supper.

But he gives only one instance in which presbyters ordained, and that is a matter of inference rather a historical record of an act actually performed. He speaks of the great bishop of Carthage, Cyprian, who was exiled from his church, and on one occasion for as long a period as two years. In his enforced absence he wrote to his clergy, exhorting and commanding them that 'in his stead they should perform those offices which "the Ecclesiastical Dispensation (*Administratio religiosa*)" requires'. King argues that in so long an absence men would come forward for ordination, and the bishop therefore must have authorized the presbyters to act for himself in ordaining.

So when the Fathers say that the Presbyters performed the whole office of the Bishop, it naturally ensues that they confirmed, ordained, baptized, etc.

But it should be observed that in the example given of ordination by presbyters, it was with the permission—nay, by the command of the bishop.

On Wesley's behalf, it may be urged that in this Primitive Church envisaged by King, there always was a bishop. But what is to be done by a presbyter when there is no bishop? That was the case of North America.

Here there are bishops: in America there are none, neither any parish ministers. So that for some hundred miles together there is none either to baptize or to administer the Lord's Supper. Here, therefore, my scruples are at an end.

Wesley might have argued: 'Lord King has proved to me that presbyters have inherently the right of ordination, but that this right can be exercised in ordinary circumstances only by the bishop's authority and permission. In North America, however, the circumstances are extraordinary, for there is no bishop. I, therefore, must exercise the right which is inherent in me for the benefit of those who are without minister or sacrament.'

If only King had been free to quote 'the mysterious person known as Ambrosiaster, contemporary with Jerome' (and had Wesley too known of him) 'In Alexandria and throughout the whole of Egypt, if there is no Bishop, a Presbyter consecrates'[3] —it would have been as honey in Wesley's mouth.

Our conclusion then, is this that King's book does not justify Wesley's consecration of Coke. It is only by taking the case of North America out of the circumstances of the Primitive Church, as described by King, and regarding it as one not contemplated by King, for which he makes no provision, that Wesley's action can be understood and approved.

But are there no other precedents for ordination by a presbyter than those allowed by King? Though Wesley does not mention it in his letter to America, we know that he cited in defence of his proceedings 'the practice of the Church of Alexandria for two centuries'. Both the biographers of Coke, Drew and Etheridge, refer to this in their account of Wesley's interview with Coke at which the plan for America was put before him. Drew says that Wesley took Coke aside into his study in the little house at City Road (still standing just as it was in Wesley's day).

In the month of February, 1784, he [Wesley] called Dr Coke into his private chamber, and after some preliminary observations introduced the important subject to him in the following manner—

'That as the Revolution in America had separated the United States from the Mother Country and the Episcopal Establishment was utterly abolished, the Societies had been represented to him in a most deplorable condition; that an appeal had been made to him through Mr Asbury. . . . He intended to adopt a plan as closely to the Bible as possible, his eye upon the conduct of the Primitive Churches in the age of unadulterated Christianity. He had much admired the mode of ordaining its bishops which the Church of Alexandria had practised. . . . The presbyters of that venerable apostolic Church exercised the right of ordaining another from their own body by the laying on of their own hands, and that this practice

---

[3] '*In Alexandria et per totum Aegyptum, si desit episcopus, consecrat presbyter.*'

continued among them for 200 years till the days of Dionysius. And finally that being himself a presbyter, he wished Dr Coke to accept ordination from his hands and to proceed in that character so to superintend the Societies in the United States.'

It has also to be remembered that when Dr Coke, in his character as superintendent or bishop, ordained Asbury in December 1784, at Baltimore, first as deacon and elder and finally as superintendent, he spoke of this Alexandrian precedent. It may seem surprising that there is no mention of it in King's book. King only refers to Alexandria as a seeming exception to his statement that the diocese was limited in size to the city parish. He allows that Alexandria was a very great city and the number of Christians there was large, and therefore in the outlying and distant suburbs Christian centres of worship were established; but still it remained true, even for Alexandria, that on great occasions all the Christians could assemble in one church as one congregation. There is no allusion to an Alexandrian practice of the consecration of the bishop by the presbyters. The explanation of this is simple and obvious. In King's time the chief, almost the sole, proof of this practice was the passage from Jerome.

For at Alexandria from the time of Mark the evangelist down to Bishops Heraclas and Dionysius, the Presbyters were always naming (hailing) as Bishop one elected from themselves and placed in the higher grade.[4]

But King limited his patristic authors strictly to the first three centuries: the only exception he allowed was Eusebius, who was of the fourth century, because he was a historian. Jerome did not belong to King's panel of authorities.

We need not look farther than Stillingfleet's *Irenicum* for the source of Wesley's knowledge of Alexandria. Stillingfleet not only quoted Jerome's sentence, but also discussed its implications at length. Bishop Gore was disposed to challenge the accuracy of Jerome—he thought that Jerome might be in error. But the Master of Selwyn College, Dr Telfer, has collected all the corroborative evidence in Greek, Latin, Arabic and Coptic writers in an article, published in *The*

[4] '*Nam et Alexandriae a Marco evangelista usque ad Heraclam et Dionysium episcopos, presbyteri semper unum ex se electum, in excelsiori gradu collocatum, episcopum nominabant.*'

Journal of Ecclesiastical History (April 1952). Dr Telfer is convinced that Jerome was right, and that 'there is no longer room for doubt that early Popes of Alexandria took office without the intervention of bishops of other sees'—that is by presbyteral appointment.

Now, though Stillingfleet does not know all Dr Telfer's witnesses, brought into court in support of Jerome by modern research, yet he is acquainted with one of the chief of them, Eutychius, through 'our most learned Selden'. Eutychius, the Melchite patriarch of Alexandria, wrote his *Annals* in Arabic, and he told the story that before he died the Bishop Mark appointed twelve presbyters to choose one of their number as his successor and set him on the episcopal throne. This method seems to have persisted for many years: for in turbulent Alexandria it was peculiarly necessary that there should be no doubt about the succession, and no long interval between one bishop or pope and another.

The evidence, therefore, of antiquity is that certain representative presbyters—recognized alike by the congregation, the body of presbyters and the bishop—had the responsibility for electing and consecrating the bishop in the Church of Alexandria. Is this a method of ordination or consecration which lends any sanction to Wesley's proceedings? Dr Coke comes down to Bristol with James Creighton, another presbyter of the Church of England, and the three of them ordain in a private room two of Wesley's preachers, Whatcoat and Vasey—on one day as deacons and on the next day as presbyters. Could these three presbyters claim to be in any sense or degree representatives of the Church of England in what they did—of the body of its presbyters or of its bishops? They were three individuals acting without authorization from the clergy or bishops. They were ordaining without the knowledge or consent of a bishop, being ministers of a Church in which, in the clearest manner, the presence and act of a bishop were made essential to ordination. This objection lies even more heavily against Wesley's subsequent consecration of Coke with the assistance of one presbyter of the Church of England and the two newly ordained elders. I do not think that Alexandria can be stretched to cover Bristol.

However, something more has to be said. Stillingfleet's general view of the organization of the Primitive Church was that it was derived from the synagogue. Originally every elder in the synagogue might lay hands upon a disciple and make him elder; but since this power was found to lead to disorder and laxity, it was made subject to restraint by a college of elders with its president—the Ruler of the Synagogue. Similarly in the Church, writes Stillingfleet:

Every Presbyter and Presbyters did ordain indifferently, and thence arose schisms: therefore the liberty was restrained and reserved peculiarly to some persons who did act in the several Presbyteries . . . without whose presence no ordination in the Church was to be looked on as regular.

The main controversy is when this restraint began and by whose act, whether by any act of the Apostles, or only by the prudence of the Church itself. But in order to our peace, I see no such necessity of deciding it, both parties granting that in the Church such restraint was laid upon its liberty of ordaining Presbyters: and the exercise of that power may be restrained still, granting it to be radically and intrinsically in them.

For those that are for ordinations only by a Superior order in the Church, acknowledging a radical power for ordination in Presbyters, *which may be exercised in case of necessity*,[5] do thereby make it evident that none, who grant that, do think that any positive Law of God hath forbidden Presbyters the power of ordination, for then it must be wholly unlawful and so in case of necessity it cannot be valid.

Which doctrine I dare with some confidence assert to be strange to our Church of England, as shall be largely made appear afterwards.

This was the voice of one who came to great honour and authority in the Church of England—as preacher, councillor, and bishop. We cannot do justice to Wesley, except we put ourselves in the environment of the religious thinking of his age. King said that the power to ordain was inherent in the presbyter, but could not be exercised without the consent of the bishop. Stillingfleet says that this power was 'radical' and 'intrinsic' in the presbyter, and he goes beyond King in contemplating the possibility of its use without a bishop *in case of necessity*—no Law of God or of the Church of England forbidding. As Wesley pondered the distressful plight of the American Methodists, that appeared to him to be a most urgent *case of necessity*.

[5] The italics are mine.

C

CHAPTER IV

LOVE OF THE CHURCH OF ENGLAND

WE come now to the third element in Wesley's church-manship—his warm attachment to the Church of England. This is abundantly manifested, even in the manner and circumstances of his appointment of Coke as Superintendent in America—so irregular and opposed to the order of the Church of England. In the certificate of ordination, the American Methodists are described as those 'who desire to continue under my care, and still adhere to the Doctrine and Discipline of the Church of England', and are 'greatly distrest for want of ministers to administer the Sacraments according to the usage of the said Church'. Wesley had encouraged Methodists in North America to follow the same rule as obtained in England: for preaching and fellowship they might use the Methodist Society, but for prayer and worship they were to go to the parish church.

In writing to the American brethren, he informed them that he had prepared for them 'a Liturgy little differing from that of the Church of England (I think the best constituted National Church in the world) which I advise all the travelling preachers to use on the Lord's Day in all the congregations'.

It is common among Anglicans in England today to quote the last sentences of a statement of Wesley entitled *Farther Thoughts on Separation from the Church*:

I live and die a member of the Church of England. . . . None who regard my judgement or advice will separate from it.

This statement is dated 11th December 1789. Wesley died on 2nd March 1791, so that these words may be taken as expressing almost the last desire and resolve of a very old man.

But, if we are rightly to appreciate them, we must learn what Wesley meant by the Church of England, and what he regarded as remaining within her and separating from her. The nature of his allegiance to the Church of England can only be understood after a review of his words and actions while remaining nominally a priest within her Communion. On 14th May 1760 John Wesley wrote to his brother Charles that he was at his wits' end with regard to two things. One of these was the relation of the Methodist Societies to the Church of England; and if he was in this perplexity, is it any wonder that students of the history of Methodism have felt themselves involved in the same difficulty?

Consider also the letter which Wesley wrote twenty-five years later (19th August 1785) to his aged brother, failing in health and plunged in fathomless grief by John's action in ordaining Coke:

But here another question occurs—'What is the Church of England?' It is not 'all the people of England'. Papists and Dissenters are no part thereof. It is not all the people of England except Papists and Dissenters. Then we would have a glorious Church indeed! No, according to our Twentieth Article,[1] a particular Church is 'a congregation of faithful people' (*coetus credentium*, the words in our Latin edition) 'among whom the word of God is preached and the sacraments duly administered'.[2] Here is a true logical definition, containing both the essence and the properties of a Church. What, then, according to this definition is the Church of England? Does it mean 'all the believers in England (except Papists and Dissenters) who have the word of God and the sacraments duly administered among them'? I fear this does not come up to your idea of 'The Church of England'. Well, what more do you include in that phrase? 'Why, all the believers that adhere to the doctrine and discipline established by the Convocation under Queen Elizabeth.' Nay, that discipline is well nigh vanished away, and the doctrine both you and I adhere to.[3]

This letter shows that in that age there might be very different conceptions, political and theological, of what the Church of England really was, and, as a consequence of what was meant by belonging to or separating from the Church. It will help us to distinguish two differing accounts of the Church of England. According to one it is the Church Established by Law, the Establishment, a Particular National Church. And according to the other it is a Branch in England of the Church Catholic. The one may be transient and cease to exist: the

---

[1] It should be 'Nineteenth Article'.   [2] See *supra*, p. 16, footnote 2.
[3] *Letters*, VII.284-5.

other will endure as long as time. The one is constituted by
Acts of Parliament and the assent of the Crown; and the other
draws its constitution from Scripture and tradition. One is
dependent upon a National Assembly, and the other is free
and independent, its Faith and Order being under the Holy
Spirit of its own choice and conviction.

Now the former conception was very much stronger and
more in evidence in the eighteenth century than it is today.
The Act of Uniformity of 1662 was based upon the theory
that all Englishmen ought to belong to the Church of England;
and if any Englishman did not belong, then he must be
subjected to deprivations and penalties. This Act was therefore associated with a series of penal laws—the Five Mile Act,
the Conventicle Act, the Corporation and Test Acts. From
these a partial relief was given by the Toleration Act of 1689,
by which congregations declaring themselves to be 'Protestant
Dissenters' might insure their meeting-houses against trespass
and destruction, and dissenting ministers, on taking the oaths
of allegiance, might obtain a licence to preach and might
protect their persons from arrest by the constable or from
the violence of the mob. The idea prevailed that the Government had assigned the duty of Christian instruction in each
parish solely to the man on whom the bishop had laid hands
with the words, 'Take thou authority to read the Gospel . . .
and to preach the same', or 'Be thou a faithful dispenser of the
Word of God'. Just as the village inn was the proper place for
the dispensing of ale, the parish church was the proper place
for the dispensing of Christian truth. Field preaching was not
simply an offence against the decorum of the eighteenth
century: it was a crime. It was preaching in the wrong place,
where the law did not allow. And lay preaching was even
more criminal: it was preaching by the wrong person, one
not permitted by law so to do. The people of the parish
were a legal assignment to the parson for the purposes of
religion.

This view was so general that we find it in unexpected
quarters, as for example in the mind of Samuel Walker, the
evangelical curate of Truro. Walker had what one can only
regard today as an extraordinary opinion of that which

constituted the Church of England. It was not its faith, or doctrine at all. These it derived from Christ and shared with all other orthodox Churches. What distinguished it from them and made it a particular national Church was its laws—by which Walker meant more especially the laws which Parliament, with the King's assent, had enacted about it. In 1755 a correspondence passed between Walker and his friend Thomas Adam, Rector of Wintringham, on the one side and the two Wesleys on the other upon the subject of lay preaching. John Wesley found himself in a dilemma. On the one hand, he was not sure that the laws of England would allow his lay 'Helpers' to continue their preaching, unless they turned Dissenters and separated from the Church of England—an expedient abhorrent to him. Was he to stop them? And, on the other hand, he could not but see that God was owning and abundantly blessing the labours of these men. He had no doubt that they were truly called of God. Must he not obey God, and confirm their work?

Wesley lays his difficulty before Walker and Adam. For Walker the problem does not exist at all. He dismisses the possibility that these lay men may be called of God as a sheer irrelevancy—the only question is: 'Does the Establishment allow lay preaching? Is it according to the Constitution of the Church of England, as defined by the laws of Parliament? If it is not, as it is not, then the Methodist Societies must discontinue lay preaching, or become Dissenting.'

This conception of the Church of England and this view of lay preaching is so remote from our thought today that I give a rather long extract from Walker's letters. Let him speak for himself. No Anglican today would use his arguments, for the Church of England itself now gives an honoured place to the lay preacher and is thankful to have his services in many a rural parish. We have, however, to see Methodism in its eighteenth-century setting.[4]

The essence [of the Church of England], considered as such, consists in her orders and laws, rather than in her doctrines and worship, which constitute her a Church of Christ.

[4] The complete correspondence will be found in *The Early Cornish Evangelicals*, by G. C. B. Davies.

A Particular Church is that where these things essential to the being of a Church of Christ, are executed with such appointments as are peculiar to that peculiar Church. Consequently the essence of a Particular Church is not that wherein it agrees with all the Churches of Christ, but that which is particular to itself. And so it is by submitting to these particular rites, that a man professes himself a member of that Particular Church. Whereas to depart from them is to separate from it. All that can be left to a Particular Church is to settle government and modes of worship, because all other things are settled already by Christ. If this be well considered, it appears that lay preachers, being contrary to the constitution of the Church of England, are . . . a separation from it.

It is quite another question, whether lay preachers be agreeable to the appointment of the Spirit respecting the Ministry. . . . But this is not the point. Is lay preaching agreeable with the constitution of the Church of England? . . .

The Church Establishment binds the conscience as a civil constitution, which it becomes by the authority of Government. . . .

You easily see what an impossibility there is that a ministration of the Word in a manner contrary to the Establishment should be consistent with the Establishment, where one of the two great points that constitute that practical Establishment, is its peculiar way of appointment respecting the ministration of the Word.

It must seem extraordinary that Walker, who was a good and able man, should dismiss so summarily the possibility that the Methodist lay preachers might be called of God. The explanation appears to be that, without explicitly acknowledging it even to himself, he had made up his mind that such men could not be divinely appointed ministers of the Good News of salvation. They were men of a froward disposition, of an unhumbled spirit, thinking too highly of themselves, poor judges of what they were called to confer upon, jealous and ambitious of office and authority. It was a thing incredible to Walker that God should have appointed farm labourers, artisans, small tradesmen and the like to bring back England to repentance and faith. He was of a good county family in the West, a graduate of Oxford who once had an expectation of being elected a Fellow of his College, one who with a nobleman's son had made the 'grand tour', and had been a greatly admired young man of fashion before his conversion. He is an example of Wesley's maxim that Christian goodness or perfection does not deliver a man from ignorances, prejudices, and infirmities. All his aristocratic disdain comes out in the sentence of a letter to Charles Wesley:

It has been a great fault all along to have made the low people of your council; and if there be not power enough left in your brother's hands to do as he sees fit, they will soon show him they will be their own masters.

Walker established a large religious society in Truro, but no layman ever 'expounded the Scriptures' in it: he suffered no man to speak but himself. The history of that Society is significant. After Walker's death, it became a Congregational church, which is now defunct.

But John Wesley knew his men; he knew that they were of a spirit very different from Walker's description. He had travelled in Cornwall with that noble-hearted stone-mason John Nelson, a man of native power of mind and speech, and had shared with him the bare boards of a Cornish cottage at night. Wesley had overcome 'the vehement prejudice of his education'.

On the subject of lay preaching Wesley's mind was, in the end, quite made up. He wrote to Walker: 'If we cannot stop a separation (from the Church of England) without stopping lay preachers, the case is clear—we cannot stop it at all!' There was, therefore, to Wesley in mid-career as an evangelist, one thing at least which he set before his attachment to the Church of England: it was his fellowship of labour with these lay men. He would separate from the Church rather than abandon and disown them.

So the lay preaching continued, but with what result? The main body of Methodism was driven into dissent and thrust out from the Church of England by the penal laws of the Establishment. Wesley struggled to the end of his life against this consequence. Relying on its title, he maintained that the Conventicle Act was aimed against seditious meetings, and it could not, therefore, be intended for use against the gatherings of Methodists, for they were pre-eminently a body of loyal and law-abiding subjects of His Majesty.

He actually issued from his Conference and by letter to one and another of his 'Helpers' the advice that *preaching houses* (the term *'meeting-house'* he would not allow) should be

registered without any declaration of 'Protestant Dissent',
and that the lay preachers should obtain licences simply as
'Methodist preachers'—a quite impossible procedure. But he
argued and contrived in vain.

When Methodists, charged with holding unlawful assemblies for religious purposes, pleaded that they were members
of the Church of England, the magistrates replied, 'The
benefits of the Toleration Act are available only for those who
have declared themselves to be Protestant Dissenters. If you
are Church-men, then the parson is your preacher, and the
parish church your place of meeting'; and they came down on
the Methodists with heavy fines. Two Methodist 'preaching-
houses' were destroyed by mobs without compensation. The
inevitable consequence was that Methodist trustees registered
their preaching-houses as for Protestant Dissenters, and the
lay preachers obtained protection by taking licences as
dissenting ministers.

At his Conference in 1766 Wesley framed a definition of
dissent or separation from the Church of England, which not
only satisfied him at the time but also was often used by him
in later years. In answer to the question, 'Are we not Dissenters?', he replied:

We are not *Dissenters* in the only sense which our law acknowledges:
namely, 'persons who believe it is sinful to attend the service of the
Church'; for we do attend it at all opportunities!

But what law was this? It was the law of the Establishment—
including such parliamentary enactments, for example, as the
Test Act, which excluded persons from municipal office unless
they communicated in the parish church. Wesley and those
who followed him were not 'occasional Conformists' for the
sake of gain or position: they were lovers of the Church of
England, who would have been, if allowed, devout and regular
communicants.

In 1768 Wesley was able to write to Thomas Adam, the
Wintringham rector, denying that many Methodist preachers
had obtained licences as dissenting ministers. The number of
such, he said, was very small; but it rapidly increased until it
formed a majority. Yet even in 1790, the year before his

death, Wesley could write two letters of indignant remonstrance to the Bishop of Lincoln (for registration and a licence could be obtained before a bishop as well as before the Justices of the Peace) protesting against a fine of £20 which had been inflicted on a Methodist, who was a poor man, for holding a little meeting in his house.

Does your Lordship know what the Methodists are? that many thousands of them are zealous members of the Church of England and strongly attached not only to His Majesty but to his present Ministry? . . .

The Methodists in general, my Lord, are members of the Church of England. They hold all her doctrines, attend her service, and partake of her sacraments. They do not willingly do harm to any one, but do what good they can to all. To encourage each other herein they frequently spend an hour together in prayer and mutual exhortation. Permit me then to ask, *Cui bono*, 'For what reasonable end' would your Lordship drive these people out of the Church? . . . Do you ask, 'Who drives them out of the Church?' Your Lordship does, and that in the most cruel manner—yea, and the most disingenuous manner. They desire a licence to worship God after their own conscience. Your Lordship refuses it, and then punishes them for not having a licence.'[5]

To all this one may reply that the Bishop was set to administer the law as it stood and could do no other: but it was a bad law, infamously bad, and the bishops were doing nothing to amend it. It must be recognized, therefore, that the Establishment was through parliamentary law continuously thrusting the Methodist people out of the Church of England. Wesley's argument that this law was not, in intention, directed against such persons as the Methodists who attended church, was quite ineffective and futile: it was not well found in law.

But let us consider the relation of all this to the consecration of Coke. On 13th September 1785 John Wesley wrote to his brother Charles:

I see no use of you and me disputing together; for neither of us is likely to convince the other. You say I separate from the Church. I say I do not. There let it stand.[6]

Were these two talking of the same Church, and was John Wesley's reply to his brother truly relevant and pertinent?

[5] *Letters*, VIII.209, 224.   [6] ibid., VII.288.

Charles was speaking of the Church of England as a Branch of the Church Catholic, with a constitution derived, so he believed—from Christ and His apostles, and John of a national particular Church, with a constitution defined by parliamentary laws. The appeal of Charles was to the ordinal in the Prayer Book, and John persisted in referring to the statute book.

When Charles Wesley sorrowfully accused his brother of separating from the Church of England, he meant that his brother had violated the fundamental order of the Church of England, an order which (though it had the sanction of Parliament) had not been framed by Parliament, but came out of antiquity of the Church's own choice; and in violating that order, John had indeed separated from the Church. Charles wrote to Dr Chandler:

I can scarcely yet believe it, that in his eighty-second year, my brother, my old intimate friend and companion, should have assumed the episcopal character, ordained Elders, consecrated a Bishop, and sent him to ordain our lay-Preachers in America. . . .

Lord Mansfield told me last year that Ordination was separation.[7]

John Wesley in his defence to his brother reverts to that old 1766 definition of separation—which meant merely not going to church. He wrote to Charles on 19th August 1785:

I have no more desire to separate than I had fifty years ago. I still attend all the ordinances of the Church at all opportunities; and I constantly and earnestly desire all that are connected with me so to do. When Mr Smyth[8] pressed us to 'separate from the Church', he meant 'Go to Church no more' and this was what I meant seven and twenty years ago[9] when I persuaded our brethren not to separate from the Church.

But, assuredly, allegiance to the Church of England must mean more than mere attendance at her services: it must include belief in her doctrine and obedience to her discipline. The absence of either of these is a spiritual separation, no matter how regular a man may be in his external use of the ordinances of the Church.

[7] Jackson, *Life of Charles Wesley*, II.391.
[8] The Rev. Edward Smyth, who in 1778 at a little Irish Conference held in Dublin, proposed separation from the Established Church of Ireland.
[9] At the Conference of 1757.

No charge of heresy, departure from the doctrine of the Church of England, was ever sustained against John Wesley. He always claimed, and proved too, that the characteristic doctrines of Methodism were not religious novelties: they were parts of the old, good, sound doctrine of the Church of England, taught in her *Prayer Book* and the *Homilies* and by her great divines. Wesley did but revive and restore neglected truths in Anglican teaching. Someone has spoken of the four universals of Methodism—all men have sinned and need salvation, all men may be saved through faith in Christ, all who are saved may know that they are saved, and all who are saved must go on to perfection. The last two of these universals were principally the target of attack among critics and opponents in the Church of England. They savoured of that horrid thing—'*enthusiasm*', which in the eighteenth century meant an excessive, irrational, and morbid emotionalism.

That a Christian man should affirm that he *knew* God had forgiven his sins and that the love of God was upon him, this '*perceptible* witness' of the Spirit to a man's soul, or 'perceptible' proof of being saved, was really going too far in the Age of Reason: it was transgressing the limits of the knowledge assigned to man.

One remembers how the two Wesleys called upon Dr Gibson, the Bishop of London

to answer the complaints he had heard against us, that we preached an absolute assurance of salvation. Some of his words were—'If by assurance, you mean an inward persuasion whereby a man is conscious in himself, after examining his life by the law of God, and weighing his own sincerity that he is in a state of salvation and acceptable to God, I don't see how any good Christian can be without such an assurance.' 'This', we answered, 'is what we contend for.'[10]

Wesley's definition of Christian perfection came to be very simple. It was just the love of God and man, filling and ruling the heart, and suppressing all consciously selfish and sinful impulses; it was a state which did not exclude ignorance, and infirmities. John Wesley himself never claimed to have attained it: but he was always ready to sit at the feet of any man or woman—it mattered not how lowly—who professed

[10] *Journal*, II.93.

to have found this blessedness, in order that he himself might learn more about its nature and himself come nearer to the fullness of Christian experience.

On this subject too John Wesley conversed with the Bishop:

I think it was in the latter end of the year 1740 that I had a conversation with Dr Gibson, then Bishop of London, at Whitehall. He asked me what I meant by perfection. I told him without any disguise or reserve. When I ceased speaking he said, 'Mr Wesley, if this be all you mean, publish it to all the world. If any one can confute what you say he may have free leave.' I answered, 'My Lord, I will', and accordingly wrote and published the sermon on Christian Perfection.

Wesley often referred to that conversation.[11] It was in that same period, in the early springtime of Methodist evangelism, that John and Charles saw Archbishop Potter.

He showed us great affection, . . . cautioned us . . . to forbear exceptional phrases, to keep to the doctrines of the Church. We told him . . . we would abide by the Church till her *Articles* and *Homilies* were repealed.

I think these two evangelists were true to the vows of their young manhood. What John wrote to Charles in their old age in 1785 after the consecration of Coke was a fact: 'The *Doctrine* both you and I adhere to.' There never was any separation by John Wesley from the Doctrine of the Church of England.

But obedience to the *Discipline*? That was a different matter. Where was the Discipline of the Church of England to be found? When Wesley was discussing with Walker of Truro in 1756 the laws of the Church of England, he referred to the Canons. It may be said safely that there are very few persons today in the Church of England who know what its Canon Law is, or even understand the term. For the Canon Law of the English Church is much more than the Canons of 1603 or 1604 now undergoing revision. That is a comparatively short and simple code, provided for the more pressing need of rules and regulations in the Church of England after the Reformation. But Canon Law includes also Decretals of the Popes in the medieval age and the Constitutions of

11 *Works*, XI.374; *Letters*, II.277, III.157, V.172.

Papal Legates and Provincial Synods in England in pre-Reformation times which have not been abrogated and are not 'contrary and repugnant to the King's prerogative and the customs, laws, and statutes of this Realm'. None but abysmally and eccentrically learned clerics, or lawyers specializing in ecclesiastical cases and practising in the ecclesiastical courts, have any knowledge of what these unabrogated remnants are —and even they suffer some dubiety.

We can understand, therefore, what Wesley meant when he wrote to Walker about those who in his Conference of 1755 had strongly urged separation from the Church of England:

As to the laws of the Church, if they include the Canons and Decretals, both which are received as such in our Courts, they think the latter are the very dregs of Popery and that many of the former, the Canons of 1603, are as grossly wicked as absurd. And over and above the objections which they have to several particular ones they think (1) that the spirit which they breathe is throughout truly Popish and anti-Christian; (2) that nothing can be more diabolical than the *ipso facto* ex-communication so often denounced therein; (3) that the whole method of executing these Canons, the process used in our Spiritual Courts, is too bad to be tolerated not in a Christian but in a Mohametan or Pagan nation.

Now Wesley was not recording here his own opinion of the Canon Law, but that of men whom he opposed: for he persuaded his Conference to declare that, even were it *lawful* to separate from the Church of England, it was not *expedient*. None the less we know from other passages that Wesley had a poor opinion of the Canons as a whole. It was not to them that he turned for the laws of the Church of England. These he looked for in the book which he loved and venerated—the *Book of Common Prayer*, with its *Articles* and *Rubrics*. He did not believe that it was a perfect book—such veneration he reserved for the Bible alone—and he thought that it was in considerable need of revision. Indeed there is a rather naïve illustration of the liberty which Wesley felt even in respect of the *Articles*. In the letter of 10th April 1781, addressed perhaps to the Earl of Dartmouth, he meets the accusation that 'he maintains it lawful for men to preach who are not episcopally ordained, and thereby contradicts the *Twenty-third Article*, to which he has subscribed'.

His reply is that

he subscribed it in the simplicity of his heart when he firmly believed none but Episcopal ordination valid. But Bishop Stillingfleet has since fully convinced him this was an entire mistake.

This is a rather surprising defence, because we feel Wesley might have pleaded truly that *Article XXIII* has nothing whatever to do with lay preaching. It is entitled, 'Of ministering in the Congregation', and decrees, 'It is not lawful for any man to take upon him the office of publick preaching . . . in the Congregation before he be lawfully called', and that means 'preaching in the parish church'. No Methodist lay preacher ever attempted to take his place in the pulpit of a parish church, and John Wesley himself never ascended it, except when he was invited thereto by the priest of the parish.

The 1745 Conference had addressed itself to this matter of Law. The question was: '*What are properly the laws of the Church of England?*' And the answer given ran: 'The Rubrics; and to them we submit as the ordinances of man for the Lord's sake.' There are the rubrics of the Ordinal in the *Prayer Book* together with the Preface. Let us glance at these. The Preface reads:

It is evident unto all men diligently reading the holy Scripture and ancient Authors, that from the Apostles' time there have been these Orders of Ministers in Christ's Church; Bishops, Priests, and Deacons. . . . And therefore, to the intent that these Orders may be continued, and reverently used and esteemed, in the Church of England; no man shall be accounted or taken to be a lawful Bishop, Priest, or Deacon, in the Church of England, or suffered to execute any of the said Functions, except he be called, tried, examined, and admitted thereunto, according to the Form hereafter following. . . .

And in the 'Forms following' the rubrics require that those to be admitted as priests shall be presented to the bishop; and the bishop in laying his hands upon him who is to be admitted as priest says: 'Take thou authority to preach the Word of God, and to minister the holy Sacraments. . . .' It is well known that there is more than one interpretation of the Preface. Some maintain it to mean that the Apostles themselves, under the authority given them by Christ, instituted the threefold order, that this order is of perpetual and universal obligation;

and that only those bodies which have preserved this threefold order in succession from the Apostles, the veritable 'Apostolic Ministry', are true branches of the Church of Christ, the Catholic Church—those which have it not, being outside the pale of the true Church.

But there are others, learned Anglican theologians and historians, who describe this Preface as a domestic document. It is an affirmation that the threefold order is of great antiquity and reverently to be esteemed, and that, for her part, the Church of England will have and preserve this ministry of the three orders, without pronouncing any judgement upon those who have it not or un-Churching them.

In the same way and for the same reasons, there are divers interpretations of Episcopacy in the Church of England—some holding it to be of Dominical origin through the Apostles and of the *esse*, the very being, of the Church; and others that it is an ancient institution, dating from the primitive Church, of proved and lasting utility and therefore of the *bene esse*, the well-being of the Church.

Both views are permissible in the Church of England. The late Archbishop of Canterbury, Dr Temple, made this clear. Speaking of the Preface to the Ordinal, he said:

It is there provided that admission to the Ministry of the Church of England is to be by episcopal ordination only, and this is all that the Church of England itself *demands*. Indeed our Church is often content, as in the *Preface* to the *Ordinal*, to direct what shall be done without binding upon the consciences of its obedient members any 'particular interpretation' of its requirements.

All parties in the Church of England set great store by the Episcopate: they cherish it, will not part with it, and believe that they have in it a treasure to share with the non-episcopal Churches. On any interpretation of the Preface and on any view of Episcopacy in the Church of England, ordination belongs to the office of the bishop. The priest at his ordination is given authority to preach the Word and to administer the sacraments, but the power of ordaining is withheld from him. In the discipline of the Church of England—the laws made by the Church in her own right—nothing can be plainer than this: and the priest who ordains is not an 'obedient member' of the Church. He violates her chosen and determined order, and transgresses a fundamental law. In a real sense he separates from the Church of England, and it was not enough for John Wesley to plead that he had not separated from the Church of England, because he was still ready to go to church. Such attendance may have complied with a law of the State: it did not comply with the law of the Church. Lord Mansfield and Charles Wesley were right: 'Ordination is separation.'

Methodist writers have been as candid in recognizing this as Anglicans. Tyerman has summed up the Methodist view in these words.

There can be no doubt that as a minister of Christ, Wesley had as much right to ordain as any bishop, priest or presbyter in existence: but he had no right to this as a clergyman of the Church of England, and by acting as he did, he became what he was unwilling to acknowledge, a Dissenter, a separatist from that Church. Such was the opinion of Lord Mansfield; and such was the argument of Wesley's brother. Wesley refused to acknowledge this; but feeling the impossibility of the thing, he declined to attempt to refute it. With great inconsistency, he still persisted calling himself a member of the Church of England; and, as will be seen, to the day of his death told the Methodists that, if they left the Church, they would leave him.[12]

When Wesley began his Certificate of the Ordination of Coke with 'John Wesley . . . Presbyter of the Church of England" he was resting his claim on a bad title.

The question, then, at this point is not whether John Wesley in consecrating Coke did right or wrong—was obeying the law of God or following his own devices and desires. The question is whether he was obeying the law of the Church of England and observing her discipline. The answer must be that he violated the law of his Church. Though the consecration of Coke took place in the room of a private house at Bristol, its consequences were soon widely manifested in two continents. Any faint desire or purpose that Bishop Seabury had to comprehend the Methodists in a Protestant Episcopal Church of America, in the Anglican Communion, was quickly abandoned, and a new Methodist Episcopal Church was established, which spread over the United States with amazing

[12] *The Life and Times of John Wesley*, III.448-9.

rapidity. This must have been known in England as in America. Whatever validity there may have been in Wesley's argument that what he had done was in a region where the Church of England did not exist and its law did not run, was absent from the ordinations which followed upon the consecration of Coke. Wesley proceeded to ordain men for the West Indies and Scotland, and in the last resort for service in England itself.

Why then did no authority in the Church of England take action against John Wesley? The Conference of the Methodist Church of Great Britain reserves to itself the right of ordination. It accepts candidates for training for the Ministry, puts them on probation after training, and finally authorizes their ordination. The President in the name of the Conference lays his hand on the head of the ordinand. There is no Church in Christendom in which ordination is more conspicuously the act of the whole Church. If today a Methodist minister were to presume to ordain any man, he would be brought to book at once by the Conference for transgressing the law of his Church.

One sometimes thinks that Wesley himself is the happiest illustration of his own saying about the Anglican Church in the eighteenth century, that as for its discipline, 'it was well nigh vanished away'. But reasons for inaction on the part of the Anglican Church will at once occur to the mind.

In the eighth decade of his life Wesley had become a greatly venerated person. The misrepresentations and calumnies which had gathered around his head had died away, and he stood forth as a great religious leader and social reformer: there was a halo of sainthood above his white hair. It would have been a most unwelcome and ungracious proceeding for any ecclesiastical authority to take disciplinary action against him. If a sentence of ex-communication had been passed upon him, the common sentiment—even among many who disliked and opposed his doctrine and way of life—would have been: 'If the Church of England cannot contain such as he is, so much the worse for it.' The bishops may have decided wisely—'Let this good, but erring, old man die in peace'.

D

Episcopi Anglicani semper pavidi. There is much more to be said of the best Georgian bishops than this. They were cautious and slow to move; but some of them treated Wesley with great kindness and discernment, and their delays were the delays of mature wisdom, of charity, and of a characteristic English toleration. Wesley himself acknowledged this. He spoke of the Archbishops Potter and Secker, of the Bishop of London (Dr Gibson), and 'that great man' Dr Louth, as those 'four venerable men'. At the outset of the Methodist movement, according to Wesley, Dr Gibson spoke rather testily about himself and his brother. 'Why can't these gentlemen leave the Church? Then they would do no more harm.'[13]

To this Wesley's retort was that his mission was, in the first place, to 'the lost sheep of the Church of England', that if he left the Church, there would be many in the Church who would listen to him no longer. By leaving the Church, so far from 'doing no more harm', he would 'lose the power of doing more good'. He cherished the hope that Methodism would serve as a leaven within the Church of England; and he endeavoured to form, though in vain, a fellowship of clergymen evangelically-minded like himself. It had become evident, however, to Wesley himself that events would not take this course of development.

Any discerning observer could see that the paths of the Methodist Society and the Church of England were diverging. The Conventicle Act and the Toleration Act in conjunction were driving Methodists, whether they would or not, into Dissent. But there was a spiritual principle, deeper and more potent in its operation than any parliamentary law, which was beginning to separate the Society from the Church. Wesley's division of preaching and fellowship on the one hand, and prayer and worship, with the Holy Communion, on the other hand was an unnatural and unscriptural division. If Methodists found saving truth in the ministry of the Word by their preachers and comfort in the fellowship of the class-meeting, it was right and proper that they should desire their preachers to have the full conduct of prayer and worship and

[13] *Letters,* VII.316.

that from their hands they should receive the sacred elements in the Sacrament instituted by our Lord.

Bishops who looked on and saw what was happening would draw the inevitable conclusion. There was no need for action on their part. They had only to wait and separation would come of itself. What would be the end only God could determine. If this Methodist work were of Him, it would endure: if it were of man only, it would come to naught.

APPENDIX TO CHAPTER IV

There is a highly relevant note of Wesley in his *Journal* on the Conference of 1788, which he says continued from 29th July to 6th August. He writes:

One of the most important points considered at this Conference was that of leaving the Church. The sum of the long conversation was (1) that, in a course of fifty years, we had neither premeditatedly nor willingly varied from it in one article of doctrine or discipline; (2) that we were not yet conscious of varying from it in any point of doctrine; (3) that we have in a course of years, out of necessity, not choice, slowly and warily varied in some points of discipline, by preaching in the fields, by extemporary prayer, by employing lay preachers, by forming and regulating Societies, and by holding yearly Conferences. But we did none of these things till we were convinced we could no longer omit them but at the peril of our souls.

During this Conference and on the day after, Wesley ordained seven men as deacons and elders, some for the West Indies, but the last of them, Alexander Mather, for service in England. It seems extraordinary that, in enumerating five 'variations' from the discipline of the Church of England, which were not inherently or necessarily breaches of its discipline, Wesley should have omitted to mention his ordinations, which were flagrant violations of the rules of the Anglican Church. The explanation appears to be that Wesley in the *Journal* was recording only the proceedings of the Conference. The five variations mentioned above were acts of the Conference, courses of action of which the Conference approved, in which it participated and persisted. But the ordinations were Wesley's individual acts, for which the Conference was not consulted, and which it did not approve. These ordinations did not take place within the sessions of the Conference, during Conference hours, but usually at the early morning hour of 4 or 4.30. They are not recorded in the *Journal*, but often only in Wesley's Diary.

It is interesting to note that a few months later, when Wesley was preaching at Cork on 4th May 1789, he alluded to the same five variations with only a difference in order and phrase. And he then said:

I hold all the doctrines of the Church of England. I love her liturgy. I approve her plan of discipline. I do not knowingly vary from any rule of the Church, unless in those few circumstances where I judge, and as far as I judge, there is an *absolute necessity*. . . .[14]

Put these two principles together. First, I will not separate from the Church; yet Secondly, *in cases of necessity*, I will vary from it (both of which I have constantly and openly avowed for upwards of fifty years). . . . I have been true to my profession from 1730 to this date.

It is harder to justify the words of Wesley on this occasion, for he was speaking of his own practice and rebuking some of his lay preachers for assuming the right to administer the sacraments. He reminded them that by the usage of the Roman, the Anglican, and the Presbyterian Churches, it was necessary for the authority of the Church to be given for this function of the priesthood. Surely it would have been becoming for Wesley to have acknowledged how far his principle of *Necessity* had carried him beyond obedience to the rule of the Anglican Church, and that he had taken to himself a power of consecration which his Church did not allow.

[14] Italics mine.

CHAPTER V

WESLEY: APOSTOLIC MAN

LET us summarize the conclusions we have reached in this inquiry. Wesley was convinced that there is no determinate plan for Church government in Scripture. Our Lord, he thought, never prescribed an order which was to be observed always and everywhere, and the scanty records in the New Testament do not exhibit a uniform and invariable pattern of organization which is divinely approved and must be maintained in obedience to the Head of the Church and His Apostles.

For the history and precedents of the Primitive Church Wesley relied principally upon two writers—Peter King and Edward Stillingfleet. The former had laid down that in the Primitive Church the presbyter, of an inferior grade, had an inherent right to ordain, but that this was subject to the direction and permission of the bishop in a superior grade. King did not provide for a case where there was no bishop, and perhaps Wesley might claim that, in such a situation, the inherent right of the presbyter became operative.

Stillingfleet allowed that in the earliest period of the Primitive Church, the individual presbyter did ordain, but this power was the cause of such disorders that it was put under restraint, and entrusted to the bishop. It could only be used again by the presbyter in a case of necessity. Wesley might plead that North America exhibited such necessity. Stillingfleet discusses at length the exceptional practice of the Alexandrian Church, in which for two centuries the consecration of the bishop was by presbyters: but those presbyters were representative presbyters, appointed by the bishop and accepted by the Church. Wesley and his coadjutor presbyters of the Church of England at Bristol could not claim to be representative of or authorized by the Church of England.

Stillingfleet, however, enunciated a principle of wide application that Church government was 'a mere matter of prudence regulated by the Word of God': so that while the cardinal articles of the Faith were immutable, forms of Church government were mutable. This was accepted by Wesley as a fundamental principle of his own churchmanship. He believed that organization might be changed better to do the work of God in any age. He himself preferred the Episcopal form of Church government, but did not think it to be of Divine Right. It was agreeable to Scripture, and the practice of the Apostles, but not prescribed by Scripture. The Apostolic Succession was 'a fable that no man did or could prove'.

In holding these views about Episcopacy Wesley was not untrue or disobedient to the Church of England: he was exercising a liberty of interpretation which is allowed to this day.

But the Church of England did require obedience to its threefold order in which the right to ordain was limited to the bishop. Wesley derived no right to ordain from his being a presbyter of the Church of England, and in consecrating Coke he violated her rule of order.

We come now to the crucial issue—Was he justified in so doing? Wesley, like many another in his time, laid great emphasis on the right of private judgement—the paramount importance of conscience. We have seen that he declared himself to have consecrated Coke with a good conscience and a single eye to the glory of God. His conscience was for himself a governing principle, and he allowed that conscience must also be a judge and decider for others. If a man believed Presbyterian government to be better than Episcopal, let him follow his conscience. If some members of a Methodist Society preferred Dissent to Conformity and would rather go to the meeting-house than to the parish church, let them follow their conscience. If the governors of the State or the bishops of the Established Church forbade Methodists to preach or meet together for mutual help in the Christian way, what was to be done? 'We must obey God rather than man', said Wesley, 'as conscience dictates.' It is quite obvious that when a man holds these strong views about conscience, there is always the danger of a head-on collision between him and the State or the Church. It came with the consecration of Coke. But who was right? Which was obeying God?

There is a passage in which St Paul enumerates the three great standards of human conduct—public opinion, private judgement or conscience, and the mind of God (1 Corinthians 4³⁻⁴); and he writes: 'I know nothing against myself: yet am I not hereby justified; but he that judgeth me is the Lord.' With what humility and submission to God does even the great Apostle speak of his own private judgement—his conscience. All know how various and unreliable the verdicts of the consciences of men upon themselves and their actions are. The depraved and criminal will profess, and with sincerity, that they have done nothing against their conscience—but theirs is a seared and evil conscience. Even the best of men have, like St Paul, to commit themselves in utter submission to the judgement of God. Was Wesley self-deceived and self-deluded, or may we think that God inspired and approved what he had done? We cannot attempt to answer that question without considering what manner of man Wesley was, the course of his life, and the situation in which Providence placed him.

Wesley used to say that he had had two calls to the Ministry in the Church of Christ: one was his *ordinary* call, that came to him through his ordination by the bishop; and the other was his *extraordinary* call that was given to him direct from God Himself. In his *extraordinary* call he distinguished two obligations: the first was to proclaim the good news of salvation in a wider field than a parish; and the second was to care for the souls—many more in number than the congregation of a parish—who were brought to seek for God under the preaching of himself and his Helpers.

Let us look at this first obligation. Throughout his career of evangelism Wesley was sustained by the conviction that God had called him to it and set him apart for it. It was a conviction which was invincible. No opposition and no danger could shake it. It never failed, even in hours of darkness and seasons of spiritual aridity. What has been described as his illumination took place on the night of 24th May 1738. Then he personally appropriated the blessing of God's forgiveness

and by an inner experience learned as never before the meaning for himself of the Gospel he preached. This exaltation of
spirit was followed by a period of anxious inquiry, in which he
was seeking to learn what God would have him do. Should
he return to Oxford with its opportunities for the cultivation
of his own soul in congenial spiritual converse and the devout
life? Should he undertake a cure of souls in some rural
parish? Was he to continue a ministry in London among
the Religious Societies and in such churches as would admit
him to their pulpits? Or had God some other work for him?
In the first three months of 1739 he spent many days at the
Charterhouse, his old school, where the room of the humble
Moravian brother, Agutter, served him as a retreat; or under
the winter sky he paced to and fro in the 'Wilderness', that
old pasture and orchard of the monks, in study of his Greek
Testament and fervent prayer. Almost certainly from this
haven he addressed on 20th March 1739, to his friend and
former Oxford pupil, James Hervey, that letter containing the
famous phrase by which he is best known. His lot was not to
be Oxford, or a country benefice, or the Religious Societies
in London, but a widespread proclamation of the Gospel
throughout England.

God in Scripture commands me, according to my power, to instruct
the ignorant, reform the wicked, confirm the virtuous. Man forbids
me to do this in another's parish: that is, in effect, to do it at all;
seeing I have now no parish of my own, nor probably ever shall.
Whom, then, shall I hear, God or man? 'If it be just to obey man
rather than God, judge you.' *A dispensation of the Gospel is committed to
me; and woe is me if I preach not the Gospel. . . . I look upon all the world
as my parish; thus far I mean, that in whatever part of it I am I judge it
meet, right, and my bounden duty to declare, unto all that are willing to hear,
the glad tidings of salvation. This is the work which I know God has called
me to; and sure I am that His blessing attends it.*[1]

Happy the man whose divine commission comes to him so
strong and clear!

The decisive act followed swiftly on the writing of this
letter. Two or three days later came an urgent request from
George Whitefield, entreating Wesley to take up the work
in Bristol which he (Whitefield) was laying down on his

[1] *Letters*, I.285-6. (My italics.)

departure for America. The request caused much perturbation in the Society at Fetter Lane, of which Wesley was then a member. Some feared that the end of it would be Wesley's death, for he was not in good health at the time. His brother Charles was particularly distressed, for—opening his Bible at random as was the manner in those days—he had lit upon the verse—'Son of man, behold I take away from thee the desire of thine eyes with a stroke; yet neither shalt thou mourn nor weep, neither shall thy tears run down' (Ezekiel 24[16]). A decision was taken by lot, and it was for Wesley's going. On the last day of March he arrived in Bristol, and saw the marvel of Whitefield's preaching to a vast multitude in the open-air. On 2nd April he himself preached abroad for the first time in his life to several thousands in a brickyard of the city, his text being: 'The Spirit of the Lord God is upon me, because He hath anointed me to preach the good tidings to the meek . . . to proclaim the acceptable year of the Lord' (Isaiah 61[1-2]).

On this Wesley remarks:

I could never reconcile myself at first to this strange way of preaching in the fields, of which he (Whitefield) set me an example, having been all my life (till very lately) so tenacious of every point relating to decency and order, that I should have thought the saving of souls almost a sin, if it had not been done in a church.[2]

That day Wesley crossed his Rubicon: he began a journeying for the saving of souls in Great Britain and Ireland that was to have no end until he came to the peaceful inn of death and found safe lodging at last.

Wesley knew the common experience of Christians. The heart which was so 'strangely warmed' at his Illumination soon underwent a fit of coldness: his new assurance of being forgiven was assailed by old doubts. But from that day in Bristol to the last day of his life Wesley never doubted that God commanded him to preach the Gospel to all with whom he had to do.

There is that very strange letter which he wrote his brother Charles, his most intimate and beloved *confidant*, in which he deplores an aridity of his soul: yet he declares that in the midst of it the urge of the dispensation of the Gospel

committed to him remains in unbroken strength. Remember
that this letter is dated 27th June 1766, after years of the
most fruitful evangelism. The words in square brackets are
in Wesley's shorthand:

In one of my last I was saying I do not feel the wrath of God abiding
on me; nor can I believe it does. And yet (this is the mystery) [I do
not love God. I never did]. Therefore [I never] believed in the
Christian sense of the word. Therefore [I am only an] honest heathen,
a proselyte of the Temple, one of the Φοβούμενοι τὸν Θεόν.[3] And yet to
be so employed of God! and so hedged in that I can neither get
forward nor backward! Surely there never was such an instance
before, from the beginning of the world! If I [ever have had] *that*
faith, it would not be so strange. But [I never had any] other ἔλεγχος.[4]
of the eternal or invisible world than [I have] now; and that is
[none at all], unless such as fairly shines from reason's glimmering
ray. [I have no] direct witness, I do not say that [I am a child of
God], but of anything invisible or eternal.

And yet I dare not preach otherwise than I do, either concerning
faith, or love, or justification, or perfection. And yet I find rather an
increase than a decrease of zeal for the whole work of God and every
part of it. I am Φερόμενος [5] I know not how, that I can't stand still.
I want all the world to come to ὃν οὐκ οἶδα.[6] Neither am I impelled
to this by fear of any kind. I have no more fear than love. Or if I
have [any fear, it is not that of falling] into hell but of falling into
nothing.[7]

And then this letter continues in the familiar pastoral strain.
Wesley speaks of Billy Evans—'If there is an Israelite indeed, I
think he is one'—and bids his brother in his own way to
insist everywhere on '*full* redemption, receivable by *faith*
alone!' 'Press the *instantaneous blessing*: then I shall have more
time for my peculiar calling, enforcing the *gradual* work.'

As we have said before, John Wesley was ever preaching
Christian perfection, but he never declared himself to have
reached the goal. He was ready to sit at the feet of any char-
woman or common labourer, who professed to have found
this blessing, in simple trust and the desire to attain.

What we have to observe is that the commandment to
preach to all, and the obligation it laid on John Wesley persisted through every experience—even in the darkest hours of

[3] 'Those who fear God.'   [4] 'Proof.'   [5] 'Borne along.'
[6] 'Whom I do not know.'   [7] *Letters*, V.16.

spiritual desolation. No penalty imposed by the Civil Law, and no censure or ex-communication by the Church, could turn him aside from that divinely appointed duty. To both State and Church, when they threatened to forbid, Wesley replied: 'I must obey God rather than man.'

Was his sense of the Divine Commission an hallucination, or was it a spiritual fact—something real, awesomely real, in the heavenly order? I believe that we can say without sacrilege: 'There was a man sent from God whose name was John Wesley.'

Wesley was, then, a prophet, and a great prophet: but he was also a pastor, and a most diligent and skilful pastor. He was as careful to conserve as to convert. He learned early by sad experience that those who are moved to repentance and faith in the forgiveness of God by preaching need continuous guardianship and instruction in the Christian life, without which they may fall away. His work as pastor is as notable as his work as prophet. He formed his converts into the little companies of the 'Band' or the 'Class', and these again into the larger whole of the local 'Society'. He furnished them with rules of Christian behaviour and appointed lay leaders for their guidance and comfort.

When 'Helpers' and 'Assistants' came to join him in his itinerant preaching, he drew up for them the simple and austere *Rules of a Helper*. In his tours through the country he met the Classes and Societies, went through the Society Roll and subjected each member to an examination of character and conduct, searching but kindly.

Year by year he invited the Methodist preachers, clerical and lay, to a Conference in which the character and doctrine of every man were passed under review.

In this way Wesley formed an intimate acquaintance with those who were gathered by himself and his Helpers into the fellowship and instruction of the Methodist Society.

Though his flock of Christ became a great flock, counted in tens of thousands before his death, Wesley had an amazing knowledge of the whole: he could call many of his sheep by name. The eight volumes of his letters show how wide and varied was his correspondence. He writes to some few of the great and the learned, but he writes to scores of simple and lowly men and women. He cares for their bodies as well as for their souls, and his letters are an epitome of common sense and Christian goodwill, rebuke, and affection. In this labour of shepherding he was unremitting.

If the office of a bishop may be known by its exercise, who in all England was worthier of being called a Christian bishop than John Wesley? Who among the Georgian bishops, some of them sequestered by their scholarship, could compare with Wesley in the care of the flock? He fed and tended the sheep and lambs and administered a godly discipline. He thought nothing as necessary to salvation which may not be proved out of the Holy Scriptures. He was gentle and loving to the poor, and gave all that he had or earned by his pen to relieve the wants of his preachers and the members of the Society. He was so merciful that he was not too remiss, and so ministered justice that he forgot not mercy.

Wesley had a unique and sole authority among Methodists —he never denied it nor attempted to conceal it. But he said that it came to him, not of his desiring or seeking, but by the will of God. The same God who had commanded him to preach, had also appointed him to rule!

I like very much the *Minutes* of the Conference of 1766 in which Wesley meets the objection that he assumed too much power. After explaining how the Conference had come into being through his invitation sent out to Methodist preachers, he continued:

But several gentlemen are much offended at my having so much power. My answer to them is this: I did not seek any part of this power. It came upon me unawares. But, when it was come, not daring to bury that talent, I used it to the best of my judgement. Yet I never was fond of it. I always did, and do now bear it as my burden—the burden which God lays upon me; but if you can tell me any one, or any five men, to whom I may transfer this burden, who *can* and *will* do just what I do now, I will heartily thank both them and you.

But some of your Helpers say, '*This is shackling free-born Englishmen*' and demand a *free Conference*—that is a meeting of all, wherein all things shall be determined by most votes. I answer, it is possible after my death, something of this kind may take place, but not while I live. To *me* the preachers have engaged themselves to submit, to serve me as sons in the Gospel. To *me* the people in general will submit, but they will not yet submit to any other. It is nonsense then to call my using *this power* 'shackling free-born Englishmen'. No one needs to submit to it, unless he will. . . . Every preacher and every member may leave me when he pleases; but while he chooses to stay, it is on the same terms that he joined me at first.

But this is *arbitrary power*: this is no less than making yourself a Pope. If by arbitrary power you mean a power which I exercise singly without any colleagues therein, this is certainly true: but I see no hurt in it. *Arbitrary* in this sense is a very harmless word. If you mean *unjust, unreasonable,* or *tyrannical,* then it is not true. . . . Preaching twice or thrice a day is no burden to me at all: but the care of all the preachers and all the people is a burden indeed.

Wesley, some years before his death, in fact a few weeks before his consecration of Coke—gave to his Conference of Preachers by the *Deed of Declaration,* which he drafted and registered, a 'legal specification'. By that Deed it ceased to be a gathering summoned at his pleasure and composed of those whom he invited, though Wesley was rather slow to realize this. It became a legally constituted corporate body, not dependent on the will of Wesley and continuous only with his life. More and more as time went by, it assumed an independence of its own and its decisions were made by a majority of votes. When Wesley died, it took corporately to itself Wesley's authority and did not confer this on any other single man. It did not follow Wesley's preference for Episcopacy. But this is to digress. We have to note that until 1784, John Wesley was the sole Superintendent of the Methodist Society—in America as well as in the British Isles, and he was so recognized and named by all Methodists. To Asbury he wrote that he (Asbury) might be the 'elder brother' of the American Methodists, but he (John Wesley) was their Father in God. To his brother Charles, he declared: 'I firmly believe I am a scriptural '*Ἐπίσκοπος*[8] as much as any man in England or in Europe.'[9] And even Charles was constrained to admit that this was the truth.

Those critics, therefore, of Wesley's time and later days, who object that, if Wesley could consecrate Coke, Coke also could consecrate Wesley, that the one had the same *status* and authority as the other, entirely overlook Wesley's position in

[8] 'Bishop.'   [9] *Letters,* VII.284.

the united Methodist Society. Wesley was its superintendent or bishop, and Coke was not. Wesley had an admitted and unique authority over the whole, of which Coke was void. When Wesley consecrated Coke as a Superintendent for America, he delegated to him that authority in America which he possessed; and he, and he alone, could make that delegation.

To those who would maintain that all that Wesley gave was a local Methodist superintendency in a distant branch of the Methodist Society, and not a bishopric in a Christian Church, it is possible to reply very briefly. Coke was sent out by Wesley expressly to give to the American Methodists a Christian ministry and the sacraments, or in a word to convert the Methodist Society there into what it was not yet in England, a Church of Christ with the full provision of all Christian ordinances. Stevens, the historian of American Methodism, devotes a whole chapter to refuting the charge that American Methodists misunderstood or perverted the intention of John Wesley in sending out Coke as their super-intendent, and that they wrongfully accepted him as bishop and set up under him the Methodist Episcopal Church. Stevens feels it is so baseless and absurd an accusation that it is almost unnecessary even to take notice of it, but none the less, in one long chapter and, point by point, he patiently disposes of the charge.

To me, it seems quite sufficient to say that if the difference between an ordination and a certificate of ordination had been noted, no one could ever have entertained this false supposition. Before Wesley consecrated Coke, he had drawn up three forms, based upon the forms in the Anglican Ordinal—with only some necessary modifications—for the Making of a Deacon, the Ordination of a Priest, and the Consecration of a Bishop. At Bristol he used the first two for the ordaining of Whatcoat and Vasey as deacon and elder, and then the third for the consecration of Coke as superintendent or bishop. And the same forms were used by Coke in America for the ordering of Asbury first as deacon, then as presbyter and finally as superintendent or bishop, after which Asbury received from Coke a certificate of ordination similar in wording to that given by Wesley to Coke. If anyone would know what is the substantial content of those forms, let him read the *Ordinal* of the Church of England.

Now was this action on Wesley's part necessary? Its immediate result was the separation of American Methodism from the Anglican Communion. Was it not an ill-considered and precipitate measure which Wesley need not have taken, if only he and the American Methodists had exercised a little more patience? His brother Charles thought so, for he wrote to Dr Chandler:

Had they had patience a little longer, they would have seen a real bishop in America, consecrated by three Scotch Bishops who have their consecration from the English Bishops, and are acknowledged by them as the same with themselves. There is therefore not the least difference between the members of Bishop Seabury's Church and the members of the Church of England. He told me he looked upon the Methodists in America as sound members of the Church, and was ready to ordain any of their Preachers whom he should find duly qualified. His ordinations would be indeed genuine, valid, and episcopal.[10]

Whether John Wesley was even in touch with Seabury, when he came to England we do not know. Dr Seabury was elected by a Convention of the Connecticut clergy to be consecrated as bishop. He arrived in England in 1783, and his request was declined by the Archbishop of York (there being no Archbishop of Canterbury at the time) on the ground that an oath of allegiance to the English King was required from the would-be bishop and could not be dispensed with apart from an Act of Parliament. Seabury, therefore, was driven to resort to the Scottish bishops—by three of whom he was consecrated on 14th November 1784.

But behind all this lay a long record of inaction or refusal by the Anglican authorities here. Nearly forty years earlier Archbishop Potter had urged the claims of the American Plantations to have a bishop. His successor was indifferent to this need of the colonies, and the later efforts of Archbishop Secker were frustrated. In the long history of the American colonies, no colonist could take Holy Orders without coming to England for ordination. No wonder, then, that American churchmen addressed an indignant remonstrance to England:

[10] Jackson, *Life of Charles Wesley*, II.392.

To this Church of England was our immediate application directed, earnestly requesting a bishop to collect, govern and continue our scattered, wandering and sinking Church; and great was, and continues to be, our surprise that a request so reasonable in itself, so congruous to the nature and government of that Church, and begging for the appointment, so absolutely necessary in the Church of Christ as they and we believe a bishop to be, should be refused. We hope that the successors of the Apostles in England have sufficient reasons to justify themselves to the world and to God. We, however, know of none such, nor can our imagination grant any.

Wesley himself had had experience of the unhelpfulness of the English hierarcy. Four years before, in 1780, he had applied to Dr Louth, the Bishop of London, to ordain a worthy Methodist schoolmaster for America, and had been refused. As one who in his young manhood had been a clergyman in Georgia, he had some personal acquaintance with conditions in the Church of England in the American colonies, and cannot have been ignorant of the long frustration of the desires of American churchmen. If he knew of the coming of Seabury to England in 1783, he may also have been aware of the failure of his effort to secure consecration from York, but the application to the Scottish non-juror bishops probably was not known to him. It came rather as a surprise to everybody. The consecration of Seabury in Aberdeen in November 1784, two months after Wesley's consecration of Coke in Bristol, was an unforeseen event.

Wesley's words on the inaction of the English bishops are mild indeed, compared with the remonstrance of the American clergy. He wrote to the Brethren in America:

It has, indeed, been proposed to desire the English bishops to ordain part of our preachers for America. But to this I object. . . . If they consented, we know the slowness of their proceedings: but the matter admits of no delay.

Yet, even if the English bishops or the American bishops— Dr Seabury and his two fellows, two years later consecrated by Canterbury—had consented to ordain a. few selected American Methodist preachers, the method would never have worked. The difference between American Methodists and those who adhered to the Protestant Episcopal Church of America went deeper than the difference between English

Methodists and the Church of England—it was a difference in social rank and in political loyalties and ties and above all in the emphasis which was laid upon parts of the Christian religion. If the Church of England in the eighteenth century could not contain or direct the spiritual forces of the Methodist movement in England, still less could the Church of the Anglican Communion in America make use of those forces with advantage to both. The Methodist Church there was in its first period a Church of ardent and fearless evangelism, which penetrated the forests and pioneer regions of the Republic. Its bishops and ministers were the tireless circuit-riders and its place of assembly was often the camp-meeting. The Protestant Episcopal Church in America could have smothered these fires: it could not have fed the flame.

John Wesley wrote wisely:

If they [the bishops] would ordain them [the Methodist preachers] now, they would likewise expect to govern them. But how grievously this would entangle us.

As our American brethren are now totally disentangled from the State and from the English hierarchy, we dare not entangle them again either with the one or the other. They are now at full liberty simply to follow the Scriptures and the Primitive Church. And we judge it best that they should stand fast in that liberty wherewith God has so strangely made them free.

There can be no reasonable doubt, therefore, that in consecrating Coke, John Wesley had in view the establishment of an Episcopal Church Government among the Methodists of the United States: but an unfortunate letter which Wesley wrote to Asbury has been used to question this intention. I say 'unfortunate', because it wounded the feelings of Asbury and has led to some misunderstanding on the part of others. It is dated 20th September 1788, when the Methodist Episcopal Church had been in existence for nearly four years, and was getting into its stride:

But, in one point, my dear brother, I am a little afraid both the Doctor [Coke] and you differ from me. I study to be little: you study to be great. I creep: you strut along. I found a school: you a college, nay, and call it after your own names [Cokesbury]. . . . One instance of this, of your greatness, has given me great concern. How can you, how dare you suffer yourself to be called Bishop. I shudder, I start

E

at the very thought! Men may call me a knave or a fool, a rascal, a scoundrel, and I am content. But they shall never by my consent, call me 'Bishop'!

The serious part of this letter is—'O beware, do not seek to be something. Let me be nothing, and "Christ be all in all!" '

The explanation of this letter seems to be simple. No one has ever written an article on Wesley's humour: he had some, though it was at times rather heavy-handed. Some of those terse remarks of his, recorded in the *Minutes* of his Conferences, come down so unexpectedly and with such aptness upon a situation that they must have been received with a gust of laughter by his serious-minded preachers. Indeed it is on record that the grave Presbyterians in Scotland were a little shocked at John Wesley, because he occasionally interspersed his sermons with humorous anecdotes. Anyhow, when he preached his sermon on 'The Duty of Rebuking our Neighbour', and was speaking very earnestly about the proper manner of carrying it out, he said:

There are some exceptions to this general rule of reproving seriously. There are some cases, wherein, as a good judge of human nature observes, *Ridiculeum acri fortius*.[11] A little well-placed raillery will pierce deeper than solid argument.

Are we to infer from this letter that Wesley was opposed to university education, because he made some objection to the use of the word 'college'—this man who set an impossible standard of scholarship for the English clergy and framed its monstrous regimen of study for his Kingswood school? Can we base on this letter a supposition that Wesley never intended Episcopacy in America, because he chided Asbury for accepting the name of bishop? It was the name only, and not the office that he disliked. He had before him what the title of 'Bishop' meant in England—a great salary, a palace and retinue of servants, a place in fashionable society, the pomp and power of a Lord Spiritual. Wesley did not desire that any of these accidents or perquisites should attach to the Methodist bishops. But he need not have worried: there was no occasion for him to use either ridicule or serious speech. Poor Asbury

[11] Ridicule is stronger than severity.

at this time 'could scarce command his one coat, and his yearly allowance', small enough in all conscience!

I do not think Wesley's raillery was well-timed in this instance. It is always dangerous to jest, when the jest has to be carried three thousand miles across the ocean. By the time it arrives the flavour of humour has evaporated. The reader of the letter does not see the gleam of amusement beneath the writer's eyebrows, nor the smile around his lips. This letter was 'a bitter pill' to Asbury from his 'greatest friend'. Wesley wanted no ostentation or worldly grandeur in the American 'Superintendency'. Happily the American Methodists had more sense and a better taste in choosing a title for the Episcopal office. They appended a note to the *Minutes* of their first Conference:

As the translators of the version of our Bible have used the English word *Bishop* instead of Superintendent, it has been thought by us that it would appear more scriptural to adopt their word *Bishop*.

Wesley used the Saxon term *overseer*, the Latin *superintendent*, the Greek *bishop* as synonymous; he meant by them all the same office in the Church of Christ, and it was his intention that this office should be instituted among the American Methodists who called it by its best name, saying:

At this Conference (the first at Baltimore in 1784) we formed ourselves into an independent Church, and following the counsel of Mr John Wesley, who recommended the Episcopal mode of Church government, we thought it best to become an Episcopal Church, making the Episcopal office elective, and the elected Superintendent or Bishop amenable to the body of ministers and preachers.

If there is anything certain in the government of the Primitive Church, it is that the effective election of the people was essential to the appointment of the bishop. The evidence for this in the Apostolic Fathers and other writings of their age is strong. And it is worthy of note that this element was not wanting in America in the appointment of the Methodist bishops. Coke became a superintendent only after he had been received as such by the unanimous vote of the General Conference. Asbury only consented to receive consecration from the hands of Coke after the Conference had given similarly its complete assent. There is a significant phrase which may be found more than once in the early *Minutes* of the American Conferences—'Unanimous Suffrages', as for example in 1790.

Ques. Who have been elected by the unanimous suffrages of the General Conference to superintend the Methodist Episcopal Church?

Ans. Thomas Coke, Francis Asbury.

Admitting, therefore, that beyond doubt it was the intention of Wesley in laying hands upon Coke to make him a simple scriptural bishop with the power of ordaining others to the Ministry in a Church of Christ, can we say that Wesley did right—was he moved to this action by God, and had he the approval of God in it?

Some would give a very short answer to this question. They would say that the bishopric is an office which was lodged by our Lord Himself in the Apostles, with a commandment that they should impart it to others by the laying on of their hands and that these in their turn similarly passed on the office to those others who came after them, so that, in an unbroken succession down the centuries from the time of the Apostles, bishops have followed bishops by the imposition of the hands of bishops. The Episcopate, they would urge, comes not by way of the election of a Christian people or the choice of Church assemblies, Presbyteries and the like—from beneath as it were, by the will of men: but it descends from above— from the Head of the Church, the Apostles, and bishops duly appointed by them. And persons of this persuasion conclude that Wesley's consecration was an act of presumption and impiety of which the only result could be and was that another schismatic body was created without valid ministry or sacraments.

When we remember that the parties in this transaction were a man like John Wesley and a great company of faithful people in America, all eager and ready to do the will of their Lord, we ought to hesitate long before we come to so harsh a conclusion as this. It seems to be much opposed to and very remote from spiritual realities. One thing we certainly cannot do. We cannot convict Wesley either of inconsistency or of insincerity. His action was entirely consistent with the belief he professed about the nature of Church government and Episcopacy.

Wesley held, as he was entitled to hold in the Church of England, that the account of Episcopacy and of the development of government in the Church of Christ outlined above, is not true. He had once held it, but he held it no longer. To the Irish clergyman, James Clark, he wrote on 3rd July 1756:

As to my own judgement, I still believe 'the Episcopal form of Church government to be both scriptural and apostolical'. I mean, well agreeing with the practice and writings of the Apostles. But that it is prescribed in Scripture I do not believe. This opinion (which I once heartily espoused) I have been heartily ashamed of ever since I read Dr Stillingfleet's *Irenicon*. I think he has unanswerably proved that neither Christ nor his Apostles prescribed any particular form of Church government, and that the plea for the divine right of Episcopacy was never heard of in the primitive Church.

And therein Wesley does not misrepresent Stillingfleet, whose opinion is shared by Anglican bishops and scholars of our own day.

We must complete a quotation from that letter to his brother Charles, of 19th August 1785, from which a sentence has already been taken:

I firmly believe I am a scriptural *Episcopos* as much as any man in England or in Europe; for the *uninterrupted succession* I know to be a fable which no man did or can prove.

No man in orders in the Church of England can be arraigned and condemned for holding Wesley's view of Episcopacy: it is one among the several interpretations of Episcopacy which are allowed. When Wesley consecrated Coke, he did not contravene his own belief about Episcopacy; but, because the Church of England confined the function of ordination to the bishop, he transgressed the rule of his Church, and his error was that he refused to recognize this.

That Wesley acted with sincerity we cannot doubt. There is in the beginning of his certificate of ordination the confidence of one who is acting according to conscience.

Know all men that I, John Wesley, think myself to be providentially called at this time to set apart some persons for the work of the Ministry in America. And, therefore, under the protection of Almighty God, and with a single eye to His glory, I have this day set apart as a Superintendent by the imposition of my hands . . . Thomas Coke.

'A single eye' is a recurring phrase with the Wesleys. It comes in the hymns of Charles, and is often found in the writings of John Wesley. He made it the title and subject of a sermon, but one of its earliest uses is in the letter he wrote his father, declining the living at Epworth, where it is accompanied by a full definition of the term.

I entirely agree that 'the glory of God and the different degrees of promoting it are to be our sole consideration and direction in the choice of any course of life.' . . . I do not say the glory of God is to be my first or my principal consideration, but my only one: since all that are not implied in this are absolutely of no weight: in presence of this they all vanish away; they are less than the small dust of the balance.

And indeed, till all other considerations were set aside, I could never come to any clear determination; till *my eye was single*, my whole mind was full of darkness. . . . Whereas so long as I can keep *my eye single* and steadily fixed on the glory of God, I have no more doubt of the way wherein I should go, than of the shining of the sun at noonday.[12]

The choice in 1734 by the young Wesley was between a college life and becoming the Rector of a parish: fifty years later it was between ordaining or not ordaining ministers for America. In both cases Wesley believed that he acted 'with a single eye for God's glory'. Was he self-deceived? Did God suffer this so faithful servant of His to be given up to a delusion and a lie?

I think that John Wesley became a truly happy man—not in the sense that he knew no tribulations or sorrows, for there were many of these in his life, but in the sense that he had what we call today an integrated personality, and so was possessed of a deep abiding peace and joy. By the training of his mother and his long-practised self-discipline, with the help of the Holy Spirit, he had attained to an instant and constant obedience to what he felt to be the will of God and his duty. For him to believe that a thing was right was immediately to do it. There was no split personality within him—no

12 *Letters*, I.167.

repression of the better part of his nature by the worse. No diffidence or cowardice thwarted or impaired his witness to Christ. He introduced his Gospel message naturally and with faithfulness wherever he went and in whatever company he found himself—on the road or at the inn, in the coach or on the packet-boat, with the rude and ignorant or in polite society, among peasants and artisans or with noblemen and bishops. It was his set purpose and consuming passion to present Christ to men and women who were perishing for lack of knowing and obeying Him. To this service he dedicated all that he had and all that he got and measured out and redeemed every portion of his time.

In a manner of speaking Wesley was a very uncomfortable man to meet. Dr Johnson, who loved to stretch his legs beneath a table and to pursue a good conversation to its conclusion, found him such, for Wesley would rise up before the talk was half ended to meet some engagement in his Master's business. He was a very disturbing person to Parson Woodforde, who was a decent, moral, and very well-meaning English gentleman, though he followed with very vague and faint hopes his parishioners departed this life, and recorded with more interest and zest his daily gargantuan dinners than his infrequent celebrations of Holy Communion. Wesley was wholly devoted to the promulgation in all men, high and low, of vital, inward, practical religion.

He had his infirmities and faults. By reason of these did the Holy Spirit leave him to commit a sin of presumption and sacrilege, when he was looking on American Methodism 'with a single eye to God's glory'?

It is impossible to believe that a servant of God so earnestly seeking to know His will and resolved to do it, and a company of Christian people so desirous of keeping the commandments of their redeeming Lord were left without divine guidance. No valid consecration is from beneath, from man alone; every true consecration is from above, from God in heaven. Where Christ is and where the Holy Spirit is, there is the Church. God leaves His faithful people free, under His inspiration, to choose that form of Church government which will best do the work of God among them in their day and

generation. It is primarily and principally in this spiritual
or religious sense—and not in the political sense—that a
Methodist Church is a Free Church.

There is a passage of simplicity and beauty in the first
Chapter of the *Report of the Archbishop's Commission on Canon
Law*. It serves as a preamble to a Code of Law and reads:

The Church exists to help men to follow out the way of faith and the
way of life which our Lord brought to this world, and in the finding
of which men realize the meaning of true happiness. . . . Our Lord
did not lay down a mass of rules as to how the Church was to carry
on its work. By virtue of our Lord's commission to the Apostles, the
Church itself in every generation has made what rules have been
necessary for the guidance of its life: rules, as Hooker says, drawn
from the laws of nature and of God, by discourse of reason aided
with the influence of divine grace, and over and above those that are
contained in the Bible. The Church has no authority from our Lord
to alter the way of faith and the way of life and the sacraments which
He has entrusted to its care. It cannot make a rule that Christians
need no longer believe in our Lord's bodily Resurrection, or come to
the Holy Communion; but can very well make rules so as to ensure
that every member of the Church is confronted with the fact of the
Resurrection, and that the Holy Communion is reverently administered. The Church has, in fact, authority to make only such
rules as will further its purpose as an institution for the help of men
in the following of our Lord.

Wesley would have given to this statement his whole-hearted
assent, and Methodists today may receive it with devout
thanksgiving. They may hope and believe that for some
Anglicans and themselves it has the same all-embracing
meaning; even though for others, and perhaps for the authors
of this *Report*, in the commission of our Lord to His apostles
were included, as unalterable rules, the threefold Ministry
and ordination by the bishop.

Sometimes the true Church of Christ seems to me to have
been gathered up into one man. The Church was in St Paul
at Antioch and not in St Peter and the Judaizers (Galatians
2^{11}). The Church was in Athanasius and not in the whole
Christian world, including the Bishop of Rome, which was
going Arian. The Church was in Martin Luther at the
Reformation and not in the vast confederacy of Pope, Bishops,
and Princes. And so it happened, on that occasion—lesser,

but still great—when Wesley had to take a decision for the Christian way of life in a growing nation. The true Church for that purpose was then in him, and not in the Georgian bishops.

However that may be, since Hooker has been mentioned above, let us recall the test that he put forward for a non-episcopal ordination—confirmation by results. Charles Wesley in sorrow anticipated the most lamentable results from the consecration of Coke:

What will become of those poor sheep in the wilderness, the American Methodists? How have they been betrayed into a separation from the Church of England! . . . But what are your poor Methodists now? Only a new sect of Presbyterians. And, after my brother's death, which is now so near, what will be their end? They will lose all their influence and importance; they will turn aside to vain janglings; they will settle again upon their lees; and, like other sects of Dissenters, come to nothing.

Hardly an exact anticipation of the future of the Methodist Episcopal Church!

But Hooker wrote:

Whereas some do infer that no ordination can stand but only such as is made by Bishops, which have had their ordination likewise by other Bishops before them, till we come to the very Apostles of Christ themselves. . . . To this we answer that there may be sometimes very just and sufficient reason to allow ordination made without a Bishop. The whole Church visible being the true original subject of all power, it hath not ordinarily allowed any other than Bishops alone to ordain: howbeit, as the ordinary course is ordinarily in all things to be observed, so it may be in some cases not unnecessary that we decline from the ordinary ways. Men may be extraordinarily, yet allowably, two ways admitted unto spiritual functions in the Church. One is, when God himself doth of himself raise up any whose labour he useth without requiring that men should authorize them; but then he doth ratify their calling by manifold signs and tokens himself, from Heaven; and thus even such as believed not our Saviour's teaching, did yet acknowledge him a lawful teacher sent from God; *Thou art a teacher sent from God, otherwise none could do these things which Thou dost.*[13]

Wesley was not authorized by men to consecrate Coke: he was extraordinarily admitted by God to a spiritual function of the Church. And God did ratify his act by manifest signs

[13] *The Ecclesiastical Polity*, Book VII, 14.

and tokens from heaven. The Methodist Episcopal Church of America is the most signal demonstration in history of Hooker's principle—the test by results or fruits. This Church today numbers nearly fifteen million adherents. It is the second largest Protestant denomination in the United States with a membership greatly exceeding that of the Protestant Episcopal Church in the Anglican Communion. Three years ago it was able to offer hospitality to the World Council of Churches in its University city of Evanston.

When Lambeth sent out its first Appeal to Churches outside the Anglican Communion it said that there was no call to them to repudiate their spiritual ancestry. As American Methodists cannot deny their spiritual parentage, so they have no need to be ashamed of it. He who was their Father-in-God was a man sent from God to proclaim the good news of salvation and to rule within the Church of God— an *Apostolic Man.*

CHAPTER VI

AFTER THE SEPARATION, WHAT?

SOME may think that John Wesley's rendering of the Christian religion was of an intensely, almost exclusively individualistic type. He was chiefly concerned to get men and women safely landed in heaven. He spent himself in delivering them from the bondage of their transgressions and setting them free in a state of salvation. It may be said that the corporate aspect of Christianity as the building up of a great Society upon earth, the Church, did not present itself to Wesley's vision. He was content, for example, that there should be Churches of many denominations—in England the Presbyterian, the Independent, and the Episcopalian; and on the Continent, the Roman, the Lutheran, the Reformed, and Moravian—but the necessity for there being one Catholic Church, of which all these were parts in full communion with one another was not constantly and urgently in his prayers. Indeed, it may be argued that he regarded these divisions with a measure of approval. They had been provided by God with a view to the 'necessary variety'. Christian men are not all made alike, and some have a preference for one form of Church government and mode of worship, and some for another. In the variety of Churches the need is met of the variety of human dispositions. When John Wesley met a Presbyterian or a Dissenter or a Roman Catholic, what he wanted to know was whether the man loved God with all his heart, and loved his fellow men and was trying to do them all the good he could. If the man was such, Wesley stretched out his hand and said: 'Thine heart is as my heart: give me thy hand.' This, according to Wesley, was the Catholic spirit: an inward, vital and practical religion of love was the essence of Christianity, and to possess it was catholicity.

It is easy to dwell upon the individualism of Wesley's conception of the Christian religion and to overlook his emphasis on the Christian society—the Church. No religious teacher ever laid more stress by his word and practice on the necessity for the Christian of fellowship or communion. There is the story of the young Wesley leaving Oxford and taking a long journey to obtain ghostly counsel from a serious man, who said to him:

Sir, you are to serve God and go to heaven. Remember you cannot serve Him alone; you must therefore find companions or make them. The Bible knows nothing of solitary religion.

Wesley never forgot that advice. He repeated it in his old age to his young correspondent, Frances Godfrey:

It gives me pleasure, my dear Fanny, to hear that you still continue in the good way. . . . I hope you find satisfaction likewise in some of your Christian companions. It is a blessed thing to have fellow travellers to the new Jerusalem. If you cannot find any, you must make them; for none can travel on that road alone.[1]

This was the reason for Wesley's Methodist 'Classes' and Societies, and this too was why he insisted upon the regular and frequent attendance at Holy Communion in the parish church. He had learned by experience that converts do not continue to live and do not grow in grace, unless they have the protection and the nurture of a Christian society. And in this sense he believed unfeignedly, *Extra Ecclesiam nulla salus*— 'Outside the Church no salvation'.

But the sin of the hostile divisions of Christendom did not press heavily upon the conscience of John Wesley. He was engaged primarily with sins nearer at hand and more palpable —the brutal and sensual life of the masses, the faithless and cold formalism of the professors of religion. There was no wide-spread Ecumenical Movement in his day, and in respect of it he was a child of his age. He saw the Particular Churches rather than the Church Catholic, or if he thought of the latter, it was to discover its unity solely in a religious experience—an inward unity without expression in an outward unity of organization and fellowship.

There is a somewhat curious demonstration of this defect in his churchmanship in a long *Minute* of the second Conference of 1745, which, incidentally, shows how Wesley used the terms 'overseer' and 'bishop' as equivalents.

[1] *Letters*, VIII.158.

The *Minute* is in answer to the question, which of the three Church governments—Episcopal, Presbyterian, or Independent—is most agreeable to Reason? It reads:

The plain origin of Church government seems to be this. Christ sends forth a preacher of the Gospel. Some who hear him repent and believe the Gospel; they then desire him to watch over them, to build them up in the faith, and to guide their souls in the paths of righteousness. Here, then, is an independent congregation, subject to no pastor but their own, neither liable to be controlled in things spiritual by any other man or body of men whatsoever. But soon after some from other parts, who are occasionally present while he speaks in the name of Him that sent him beseech him to come over and help them also. Knowing it to be the will of God, he complies, yet not till he has conferred with the wisest and holiest of his congregation, and with their advice appointed one who has gifts and grace to watch over the flock till his return.

If it pleases God to raise another flock in the new place, before he leaves them he does the same thing, appointing one whom God has fitted for the work to watch over their souls also. In like manner in every place where it pleases God to gather a little flock by His word, he appoints one in his absence to take the oversight of the rest, and to assist them of the ability which God giveth. These are Deacons, or servants of the Church, and look on their first pastor as their common father. And all these congregations regard him in the same light, and esteem him still as the shepherd of their souls.

These congregations are not strictly independent. They depend on one pastor, though not on each other. As these congregations increase, and as the Deacons grow in years and grace, they need other subordinate Deacons or helpers, in respect of whom, they may be called Presbyters or Elders, as their Father in the Lord may be called the Bishop or Overseer of them all.

This is a very defective account of the origin and growth of the Christian Church. Indeed one may suspect that Wesley himself was conscious of the errors and omissions in this tentative draft. It is difficult to find that the plan of development traced in it was ever put forward again; and for this reason it was not really characteristic of John Wesley. One obvious defect is that it totally fails to account for the Church Universal. Up to a point it might explain the united Methodist Society, but it is no explanation of the Catholic Church. Christ did not send forth one preacher of the Gospel, but many. The Apostles—whether we think only of the Twelve, or of that larger number who were 'Apostles of the Churches'—

were not one man, but 'the glorious company of the Apostles'. Wesley shows us only one string of churches depending from and upon one man, without indicating how this group of churches might be related to other groups—the fruits of the labour of other men sent forth by Christ. The Primitive Church certainly was not a series of strands hanging down in isolated dependence: it was, for the most part, a closely woven robe of Christ, seamless in the first centuries and only afterwards torn asunder with a rending which was heard and seen of all Christendom.

In further illustration of this defect in Wesley's thought, let me turn again to the well-known quotation from the *Journal* about Peter King's book. I have dealt with the first part already, let us look now at its concluding words which I have put in italics. This quotation is separated from the *Minute* above by only six months. The Conference was held in August 1745—Wesley read King in the saddle in January 1746:

I was ready to believe that this was a fair and impartial draught; but, if so, it would follow that bishops and presbyters are (essentially) of one Order; and that *originally every Christian congregation was a church independent of all others*.

I am quite at a loss to account for this deduction from King in the concluding phrase of Wesley: for in the context of the eighteenth century an 'Independent church' could mean none other than a Church consisting of a 'gathered congregation', which was regarded as self-contained and recognized no authority beyond itself. This was the polity of Independence, but nothing resembling it can be found in King. He devotes his last two chapters to a consideration of the independency and dependency of the Primitive Church, and its unity; but to the first of these, the independency, he gives only a paragraph or two; to the dependency and unity almost the remaining whole of the two chapters. It is true that King has drawn the picture of a diocese which was no larger than a city parish, in which all Christians could meet as one congregation. He also maintained that each parish had its full complement of ministers—bishop, presbyters and deacons together with its laity, and that each 'particular Church'; so instituted, had 'power to exercise Discipline on her own Members without the Concurrency of other Churches'. But having said so much, King immediately goes on to show how the 'particular Churches' were related to a Church Universal, so that there was a unity of the Church Universal, which consisted not in a 'Uniformity of Rites' or 'Consent to the non-essential points of Christianity', but in 'an harmonious Assent to the Essential Articles of Faith' and in an assimilation of standards of discipline.

King gave a first hint of how this unity of faith and discipline was achieved, when he said that, at the appointment of a new bishop, bishops of the 'voisinage' were consulted and called in for the ceremony of consecration; and he allowed that a particular Church which claimed to have a succession in its bishopric from an Apostle enjoyed a pre-eminent authority in matters of doctrine. Doubtless there was the precious 'deposit' of truth from the Apostles which was preserved and handed on from one generation of Christians to another; but King has nothing to say about the principal mode in which this was effected—the circulation of the Gospels and the apostolic Epistles, the gradual formation of the Canon of the New Testament.

His narrative is chiefly occupied with the story of the synods. He says that the particular Churches grouped themselves into Provinces, which held their synods at frequent intervals—sometimes to consider points of doctrine of peculiar difficulty, to correct heresy, and sometimes to deal with cases of Discipline and to heal apostasy or schism. These synods often consisted of more than bishops. Presbyters and deacons and staunch lay confessors might be members of them and prominent in their proceedings: but some synods were composed wholly of bishops, and generally they were the most influential persons in counsel, so that in the Primitive Church of the first three centuries, the bishops, beyond all others, served as the 'cement of the Church'. King hesitates to call any one of these synods a General or Ecumenical Council, representing the Church Universal—his period terminates before the first General Council of Nicæa of A.D. 325; but he

thinks that one of the latest of his period, the Council of
Antioch in A.D. 269, which tried and deposed the Bishop
Paul, Samosatenus, in size and importance came near to
being a General Council.[2]

King's picture of the primitive Church is of particular
Churches intimately related to a Church Universal—so
closely related that they were one in doctrine and becoming
one in discipline. King wrote his book to recall English
Christians to this unity. I can only understand Wesley's
comment on King, if an overriding emphasis is placed upon
the word 'originally'.

'Originally every Christian congregation was a church
independent.' Perhaps this is literally true. When a company
of hearers becomes, under the preaching of God's messenger,
for the first time a congregation of believers, for a brief period
it may have no fellowship or organic connexion with other
congregations, except through the man who brought them
the Gospel; but that stage is quickly passed. 'Independency'
was a phase soon outlived in the Primitive Church, and the
term became quite inappropriate to describe the relations
between the particular Churches of the first three centuries.

What then is the conclusion of the whole matter? In his
controversial sermon of May 1788 on 'The Ministerial
Office' the aged Wesley denied with indignation the right of
any of his lay preachers to assume the whole office of the
Christian Ministry, which included the administration of the
sacraments, or to bestow that Ministry on another. In
America, Asbury, conforming as he believed to the mind of
Wesley, persuaded the American preachers to suspend a
Resolution of their Conference of 1779, by which three
preachers were appointed a presbytery with instructions to
ordain one another and afterwards to ordain others. This
delaying action in America and the sermon at Cork go to

---

[2] It is instructive to compare King's book with Dr Gwatkin's *Early
Church History to A.D. 313*. They cover the same period, but Dr Gwatkin
differs from King in tracing more distinctly the stages in the development
of the unity of the Church. He says that the first councils of which we have
any knowledge were held about A.D. 160; and he, like King, attaches
special importance to the Council of Antioch of A.D. 269. That was a
council which removed a powerful bishop and appointed his successor
without reference to the local Church. (See Chapter 13, pp.302-11.)

prove that in Wesley's view there was a peculiar authority and sanctity in ordination by an ordained minister of the Church. If a new Church was to be brought into being, it ought to be from the old through one of its ministers. The rite of ordination must be performed with reverence and understanding by one who had been trained in study of the Scriptures, had knowledge of the history of the Church Universal, and experience in its service beyond the ordinary qualifications of the layman. In a manner, therefore, which perhaps was not perfectly defined to his own consciousness, Wesley felt that the office of a presbyter in the Church of England conferred upon him an authority which no unordained man possessed. He did not regard lightly his 'Ordinary Call', or ordination by a bishop. This had made him, so he said to Bishop Butler at Bristol, a priest in the Church of God without limitation of parish or country. It had stamped upon him, so he wrote in his *Farther Appeal to Men of Reason*, 'an indelible character'. It was fitting, therefore, that, if in America the Christian Ministry was to be conveyed to a body of professing Christians, left without a Ministry, it should come through the hands of an ordained minister of an existing and ordered Church.

Wesley did not believe that this minister must be a bishop: he thought he might be a presbyter. We have seen that the support of the ecclesiastical authorities, on whom Wesley principally relied for this assumption, is not strong. Peter King speaks of no ordination by a presbyter except with the consent of the bishop, and Stillingfleet regards presbyteral ordination as an injurious practice of the earliest period which was soon superseded, the power of ordination being restricted to the bishop, except in a case of necessity.

Wesley's authority to ordain and consecrate rests securely, not upon ancient precedents, but upon his extraordinary divine commission to preach the Gospel and to shepherd the flock of Christ. God is the great consecrator and nearness to Him—Christ is the Chief Shepherd and partaking of His mind, is what matters most in the consecrating minister. In North America a faithful minister was free to offer and a faithful people were free to accept that form of Church government which Wesley proposed. It was scriptural and rational, agreeing with Stillingfleet's cardinal principle that the form of Church government is a matter of prudence, regulated by the Word of God. The Holy Spirit and human reason concurred in Wesley's action.

This same liberty of a Christian people in the choice of Church government was exercised by the British Conference after Wesley's death. They decided not to bestow Wesley's sole authority on a single individual or a group of individuals, but to retain it for themselves as a corporate body, representative of the whole Church. In the Methodist Church of Great Britain the Conference ordains.

I should not have been afraid to talk to John Wesley about these things in spite of all my veneration for his matchless fidelity and courage—his greatness and goodness, and his white hairs. Here was one who kept an open mind and submitted to be informed and even corrected by lesser men. He would have listened to me quietly, as he listened to Henry Moore in the study and vestry at City Road. I should say to him: 'Sir, it seems to me that you do not, in all things, accurately present the views of Peter King and Edward Stillingfleet, and that you lean too much upon them. God has given to you a better title than these men, or any man, can bestow.' Of one thing I am sure, John Wesley would not interrupt in anger, or try to bear me down. He would sit there and hear me patiently to the end. And then perhaps he would be silent for a while, look at me with kindness, give me his blessing and send me on my way in peace. Or perhaps he would say: 'Yea, a dispensation of the Good News has been given to me, and a dispensation to tend and shepherd the flock of Christ. I must obey God rather than man.' So we should part in love and agreement—a Father-in-God and his son in the Gospel.

What of our own times? The Methodist Episcopal Church in India hitherto has not been conspicuous in the Reunion Movement. It has not co-operated in some of the great joint-institutions of Missions, such as the Madras Christian College: it has preferred to maintain its own collegiate and training-establishments. It had a few congregations in South India, but they did not unite with the South Indian Church. Its main strength, however, lies in the North, and now it is a leading partner there in the negotiations for Union. When this is consummated, it will bring a large body of adherents into the united Church. For them and for all who have carried on conversations with them, the nature of the American Methodist Episcopate and how rightly to deal with it have been outstanding problems. I believe that the method proposed is right, and that, in the course of time, it must have a great and wide-spread influence on the American Methodist Episcopal Church, in America as in the Asian field.

Meanwhile in England the Conference of the British Methodist Church has made important pronouncements going beyond its willing assent to the South Indian Scheme, by which its largest Church and Mission Overseas have passed into the united Church. It has declared that the breaches of unity in Christendom have been disastrous, and that our separated and aloof Denominational Churches are not according to the New Testament ideal. It believes that the existing inward unity must have its outward expression in organization and full communion. The Conference has given a sympathetic and well-considered reply to the proposal made by the Archbishop of Canterbury that the Free Churches should introduce Episcopacy into their systems, with a view to the full recognition of ministries and memberships in the Church of Christ. And now it is waiting for conversations between the representatives of the Church of England appointed by the Archbishops and representatives of the Methodist Church, appointed by the President of the Conference.

British Methodism has put forward two main conditions for full communion. First, that the same liberty of interpretation of Episcopacy shall be allowed to ministers and to members of the Methodist Church as is allowed and enjoyed within the Church of England. And secondly, that in accepting Episcopacy the Methodist Church shall not be required to forgo any measure of the fellowship it now has with other non-episcopal Churches.

Reunion is, of course, a matter of high expediency; for our divisions and our condemnations of one another are a scandal to the world, and a limitation of our powers: but that is not the chief reason for Reunion. The framers of the South India Scheme were, first and most deeply, moved by the conviction that Christ wills us to be One, after the sublime and ineffable mystery of the Triune God.

Let me close this brief essay, as Edward Stillingfleet concluded his great treatise, with the prayer:

That the Wise and Gracious God would send us one heart and one way; that He would be the Composer of our differences, and the Repairer of our breaches, that of our strange divisions and unchristian animosities, while we pretend to serve the Prince of Peace, we may at last see

THE END.